Chasing the
RAINBOW

Chasing the RAINBOW

RECURRENCES IN THE LIFE OF A SCIENTIST

by

Robert Greenler

Foreword by

Duncan T. Moore

ELTON-WOLF PUBLISHING

Seattle • Vancouver, B.C. • Milwaukee • Los Angeles • Portland

04 03 02 01 00   5 4 3 2 1

ISBN 1-58619-051-2   ISBN 1-58619-052-0 (pbk.)

Library of Congress Catalog Card Number: 00-100217

First Printing March 2000
Printed in the United States of America

Published by Elton-Wolf Publishing
Milwaukee, Wisconsin

ELTON-WOLF PUBLISHING

5630 N. Lake Drive, Milwaukee, WI 53217
414-906-0600 • e-mail: spittelman@elton-wolf.com
Seattle • Vancouver, B.C. • Milwaukee • Los Angeles • Portland

I dedicate this book to my family, who have been an important part of the life from which I have lifted the incidents comprising these essays. Barbara has been here for a long time; Lee, Karen, and Robin not quite so long; and Susan, Penny, and John, for about a decade.

I gratefully acknowledge Judy Lasca's many editorial contributions and her encouragment in the writing of this book.

RECURRENCES IN THE LIFE OF A SCIENTIST

CONTENTS

Foreword

I was thrilled when Bob Greenler asked me to write the foreword for this book. As a fellow "University of Rochester person," I knew of Bob long before I met him. Our first "real" meeting was in Leningrad (whose name would change to St. Petersburg before we left). Bob literally gave me a shirt when my luggage failed to arrive.

This was the first occasion for me to hear his lecture on atmospheric optics. After that talk I understood how his *Science Bag* lectures had become a staple in Milwaukee. Of course, I had not read this manuscript when I was approached, but I was sure that I would be delighted with it. I was not disappointed. How could I be, when a copy of his earlier book, *Rainbows, Halos, and Glories,* is still on my coffee table?

Bob is quite correct in saying that this is not an autobiography. It is a description of how scientists and engineers approach life and how we are constantly faced, like everyone, with tradeoffs. Bob has used his experiences to illustrate these sometime-difficult choices for scientists and engineers.

Spouses of technically trained people will find this book an eye-opening description of how those of us in science and technology take ordinary problems and seemingly make them into major projects. I was particularly fascinated by the "refrigerator calendar," which was built to make a cooling unit in the ground for their remote cabin but also became a calendar.

Bob has called himself a "third-rank scientist," but he has done more than many Nobel Prize winners to bring the excitement of science and engineering to everyone. His anxiety over the telephone call from an NSF contract monitor is an excellent illustration. He forced Bob to make a choice between devoting his entire professional effort to surface physics or using portions of his time for atmospheric optics and for fostering the public understanding of science. We should be thankful to Bob for making the decision to take the balanced approach.

The reader will enjoy the description of such topics as walking around the world in sixty seconds, the octellipse, and the challenges of spinning tops. Bob also discusses the support of basic research (in the *Bee Journal*) and the tradeoffs between industrial and academic research. Also of interest are his comments on the importance of summer jobs and of listening to people of all positions (whether an hourly worker or a thesis advisor), and the important role of mentors (in this case Prof. John Strong who, coincidentally, also tried to recruit me to the University of Massachusetts many years later).

Of interest to those who have ever been involved with professional societies is the section on the Optical Society of America and the proposal to create a Federation in 1987. I was on the Board of Directors at the time and still remember the way Bob handled that meeting. His fairness and respect for each person's views was very important. (It is interesting that in 1999 the same two societies debated full merger. It was accepted by the Boards of both but was rejected by members of one and accepted by members of the other.)

My stint as Associate Director for Technology in the Office of Science and Technology Policy in the White House has reaffirmed my conviction about the importance of some of the issues Bob raises in this book. Many of his examples left me thinking, "I never thought about that, but I wish I had."

You will love this book.

Duncan T. Moore

Duncan T. Moore is Kingslake Professor of Optical Engineering,
The Institute of Optics, University of Rochester, Rochester, New York

Introduction

RECURRENCES

My life is full of recurrences. Some circumstance, or idea, or physical situation brings to mind a similar event, perhaps from quite an early age. Sometimes it suggests a chain of events that seems to lead directly from the child to the adult. The clear path is seen only in looking back, however; no such orderly progression was evident along the way, and yet the path is there. The excitement of the small boy watching a rainbow must be directly connected to the excitement of the adult, standing at the South Pole forty years later, seeing the sky full of halos, sun dogs, and rainbow arcs—all produced by the tiny "diamond-dust" ice crystals glittering and sparkling in the clear, cold air. There must be some way in which the small boy followed that rainbow to the South Pole.

And there must be a connection between the eight-year-old boy in his "laboratory" producing jars of beautifully colored water or, a few years later, searching for bits of colored glass to use in his kaleidoscopes, and the adult who is the President of the Optical Society of America. Wordsworth identifies the early experience as the cause of the later effects when he says, "The child is father of the man."

I started writing this book by making a collection of "Nows" in my life, each of which suggests a "Then" preceding it by many years. In what follows you will see the "Now" described in the present tense and shown in bold-face type to separate it from the "Then" that precedes it. I made the collection without fully understanding the significance of these recurrences.

In the process I uncovered patterns in my life of which I was not aware, and I realized how much I felt myself a part of traditions through which I traced connections with people who came before me. By telling you the stories of these "Nows" and "Thens," of the patterns and the traditions, I share with you something of the nature of my life as a scientist and my view of how the human enterprise of science works

Chapter One

COLORS

Glenn and I stand in my lab, next to the sink, holding a flask in the sunlight to admire the rich, ruby red as if we are connoisseurs examining a glass of fine wine. And in a sense we are connoisseurs, taking pleasure in the beautiful liquid, watching the way it changes as we add another few drops of concentrated color. With more drops the solution loses some of its brightness, but the color deepens and becomes more saturated, glowing in the afternoon sun. Each dilution is different—and wonderful.

For me (and I suspect for many others who are visually oriented to the world) color adds interest to anything: to food, to clothing, to landscapes, and to demonstrations in physics lectures. If I have some small pieces of apparatus to be used in a lecture, how much more interesting they appear to a person coming into the room if they are displayed on brightly colored squares of felt. Sometimes a demonstration involves a glass vessel—a beaker or flask—containing water, and such demonstrations are improved, practically as well as aesthetically, by adding a vivid blue or a dramatic red color to the water.

For example, a demonstration that comes to mind involves listening to the sound of water being poured into a tall glass cylinder and hearing the tone change as the water fills the cylinder. It is the same process by which you can hear that the gas tank in your car is filling up—just before it runs over. The principle is that the noise of the splashing water contains many frequencies of sound, and the resonance of the column of air enclosed by the glass cylinder amplifies one particular frequency. That frequency is determined by the length of the air column. As water is poured into the container, the air column gets shorter and the amplified tone, heard in the noise of the falling water, rises. The level of the water is a critical part of this demonstration, and colored water is more easily seen than clear water.

So I like to use colors, and if there are several containers of water, why not use a different color for each? The easy source of these colors is the local supermarket where one can buy small bottles of food coloring. In 1976, though, something happened to the food colors: all of a sudden the red color in the set of food dyes was no longer a vibrant, rich red. At best it was sort of orange, and not a very good orange at that. What had happened was an action of the Food and Drug Administration that prohibited the use of Red Dye #2 because of suspected deleterious effects on the health of consumers. While this may have been good for consumers, it was not good for the observers of science demonstrations, and each time I added a red to enliven some demonstration, I had a small regret that it was not the red it used to be.

A few years after the prohibition of Red Dye #2 my colleague, Glenn Schmieg, who shared my "red regret," returned from England with a gift. He came to my laboratory with three bottles of food coloring from an English store. They were labeled "Ruby Red," "Scarlet," and "Cochineal." What a wonderful gift!

> **So, Glenn and I stand and savor the appearance of each of the three flasks, filled with beautiful, rich, glowing colors. In the midst of this pleasure, an incident from my childhood comes strongly to mind.**

It occurred in the summer after third or fourth grade, when I lived in the very small town of West Unity, Ohio. I found that when I touched crepe paper with wet hands, the color came off on my fingers, and when the paper was soaked in water, the color came off in the water. Crepe paper was used more in that pre-plastic era than it is now, and I found several colors of paper that produced beautiful water solutions. Out of this discovery came the laboratory that I set up against the side of the barn in our back yard.

Two up-ended orange crates supported boards that made the work bench. The orange crates provided storage shelves for the assortment of clear glass containers I collected to hold my stock solutions of crepe-paper dyes. One of my prizes was a big, round, glass coffee pot that was perfectly good except that it had lost its spout, and so nobody else wanted to use it. Maybe they didn't want it for coffee, but it was perfect for holding a big supply of deep emerald-green solution (or would it be better to store the blue in that one?). From somewhere I got a collection of small glass bottles with cork stoppers that were almost all the same size. I suppose they were pill bottles. I filled each one with a sample of color from a different jar stored below and then lined them up along the back edge of the bench. They formed a wonderful display of everything that I had in storage below.

But the real fun came from experiments of mixing my colors to produce new ones. Every experimental scientist knows that many experiments fail. In my case failure meant ending up with a color that was not pretty. The most common result from a mixture of several solutions is a color that I later named "yucck" or "the last Easter egg." But there were also successes, when the resulting color was so good that I decided to keep it. That meant making up a stock solution of the new creation and recording the recipe that produced it. And, of course, then I could represent it with a new reference sample added to the collection lined up along the back of the bench top.

You can guess that the growing number of reference vials were not randomly ordered; they ranged from the deepest red on the left through the oranges, yellows, greens, and blues to the purples on the right. This row of samples represented my collected wealth. Of course, a small vial of the liquid did not exhibit the richness and saturation of color shown by a larger container, so to really savor a color in my collection, I would have to bring up the stock solution and have another look at it—just to remember how good it really was.

I have no sense of whether this activity went on for a few days or a few weeks. I don't recall sharing it with other kids and, with one exception, I don't remember any comments made by adults about the activity. My father, who was the superintendent of the local school system, took me down to the grade school where we looked through some supply closets and found a couple of new crepe-paper colors. Certainly that represents an interest in the activity, but I don't remember any comment that he or my mother made about it. I recall it as one of the best projects I ever did as a kid and, although I would not say I had any unusual degree of self-confidence, I apparently did not require the validation of either kids or adults for me to know that it was a neat thing.

The one adult comment about my laboratory that I remember came about because my father was a beekeeper. As a young man my father had kept bees as a hobby, an activity that had expanded into a part-time job as he grew older. It was through beekeeping that I got to know Reverend Ryan, the minister of one of the small churches in our town who kept a cow and rabbits and a hive of bees. He considered my father to be his source of information on bees, calling him The Wizard for his store of knowledge on the art and science of beekeeping. I saw Reverend Ryan as a vigorous, enthusiastic, outgoing person who sang loudly, "I've come to see The Wizard . . . ," as he pounded on our back door on a Saturday morning with a bee question for my father. I had no close connection with him and I didn't know anything about his theology, but I liked him well enough.

One summer morning, when my color adventure was in full swing, Reverend Ryan was talking with my father in the back yard where I had my laboratory. Acknowledging what I was doing, the minister made a joke about it. I don't remember the exact nature of his jest, but it turned on the substitution of the word "lavatory" for "laboratory" in referring to my bench and the bottles of colored water. I remember thinking that he was wrong to make that kind of a joke at my expense. It was not right for an adult to belittle such a wonderful project

I assume that he had no malicious intent and that his joke was only thoughtless. As I think about it, I find it most interesting that his deprecating remark did not change my attitude toward my project, but only left me with the impression that he had made a mistake. That was not my usual response to adult authority at that time in my life, but this color project was something I knew was special.

Now I think that the minister made the mistake that our society makes over and over again. Young-enough children are interested in everything. Too often the process of education and socialization deadens a child's interests in one area after another. Doesn't that represent a failure of our system? The excitement of discovery and a joy in beauty are experiences that enrich a life. Creativity and originality are precious tendencies that should be treasured and nurtured, in work and in play, in child and in adult.

Now, as I stand with Glenn admiring the beautiful flask of ruby red, I think of the Then of an eight-year-old boy, and I consider some of the things that have not changed in my life. The fascination with the colors is still there.

Chapter Two

FIRST CLASS AT THE UNIVERSITY

I start the first day's lecture in the calculus class under the strong influence of my first university mathematics class as a student fourteen years ago. I introduce myself to the class, tell them a little bit about my background and that I am new to the university.

I had done some teaching when I was a graduate student but, after getting my degree, I worked in an industrial research laboratory for five years before I made the move to the University of Wisconsin-Milwaukee. Although I was joining the Physics Department, some problem of scheduling was solved if, for that first semester, I taught a calculus course in the mathematics department. It seemed a daunting experience for me to stand and face 200 students—in a math course, yet—but when the day of the first class arrived, I had spent enough time doing my homework that I was as ready as I was ever going to be.

"The fact that I am a physicist means that I am very aware of how useful this calculus is in solving interesting problems in the real world. I will work hard to help make the material interesting and understandable to you, but each of you has to do the actual learning." I write my name and office number in the upper left-hand corner of the blackboard and say that I am very willing to have them come to my office for questions or more discussion. Aside from the information contained in my comments, my purpose in making them is to indicate that I am a human being with some dimensions other than that of a mathematics teacher, and that I see a roomful of other human beings with hopes and anxieties—this I acknowledge. And now I begin with the academic subject at hand.

Fourteen years earlier I, and a roomful of other freshmen at the University of Rochester in upper New York State, sat talking and laughing nervously while awaiting the beginning of our first university class in mathematics. Most of us had done very well as high school students but had little idea of how we would fare in this new setting. Most of us in that class had aspirations in science or engineering, and the mathematics class represented a key element in fulfilling those aspirations.

The bell in the hall rang, signaling the beginning of class, but no professor appeared. A few minutes later the classroom became totally silent as we heard footsteps down the hall approaching the classroom. In strode our teacher from the door to the right of the blackboard. He was tall, thin, and expressionless. Looking neither to the left nor to the right, he passed the table in the front of the room and, on it, dropped a book. Without breaking stride he picked up a piece of chalk from the chalk tray and, as he reached the left side of the blackboard, splintered the chalk against it with the words "Consider a point!" Thus began a description of coordinate systems by which the position of that point could be specified relative to a variety of reference axes. As the discourse continued, some of us recovered enough to open our notebooks and start to record this stream of information. The stream continued until the end of the period when, with no more transition than at the beginning, he picked up his book and left, leaving behind a group of dazed students, wondering what on earth we had gotten into.

In some ways he was not a bad teacher; in fact, I would even say that in some ways he was a good teacher. He struggled to develop our understanding rather than merely leave us with a prescription for solving particular kinds of problems. He did, however, have a number of unendearing personal characteristics, including doing whatever it took to keep anyone from getting a perfect grade on any of his exams. I suppose some of these annoyances prompted student complaints to the mathematics department.

One day, after class, he called me into his office and said, "Well, Greenler, you seem to be more interested in this stuff than some of these guys. What do you think of the course?" That put it to me, but since he had asked the question, it seemed to me to be a time for truth-telling—at least time to tell some of the truth. Among other things I told him that I strongly objected to getting a B grade in his class for a level of achievement that would merit an A in any other class. He said that the only way to keep people working was to grade them down, and he seemed to ignore my claim that it didn't work that way with me.

I stayed with him in subsequent semesters, despite his classroom personality, but his classes dwindled in size as students found various excuses to transfer to other sections when they discovered who was teaching this one. Some years later, when I was a faculty member, one of my colleagues in the mathematics department was someone who had been a faculty member at Rochester in my undergraduate years. He told me that this particular person had not done well in the university and had left teaching.

I never forgot the trauma of that first class, and I vowed that, if ever I were in such a position, facing a new class of anxious students, I would spend some time affirming our common humanity before getting on with the subject matter.

So today, as a teacher in my first math class at the university, I fulfill that vow. I hope that I have been able to allay some of the students' anxieties and ease into the subject of calculus with less trauma than I experienced. The blackboard is filled with my writing, and I pause to erase it so I can continue my lecture. When I get back to that left side of the board where I had used the chalk to make my point—by writing down my name—I realize that I misspelled it. It appears that the teacher still has a bit of his own anxiety.

THE INTERNATIONAL SCIENTIFIC COMMUNITY

It is one of those early spring days that reminds me of just how wonderful an early spring day can be. The sun is shining and fruit trees are in bloom. I walk down the city street with a sense of exhilaration at being alive in a friendly world. I have no particular reason to feel so good on this day, but frequently I don't have any objective reason for feeling good—or bad. I become aware of my mood and am amazed. The city is Warsaw, in Poland, a third of a world away from the small town of West Unity, Ohio, where I grew up. My next thought is, "How on earth did Mrs. Greenler's little boy, Bobby, ever get here?"

In the town of my childhood my horizons were not distant. One year there was a much-heralded World's Fair in New York, a very long way from Ohio. I never even thought about wanting to visit it because it never occurred to me to be a possibility. I was greatly surprised to find that one of my friends was going with his family (reputed to be the richest in town) to see the fair. Travel to a foreign country, except Canada, of course, was even more unthinkable. Only very rich people could go to Europe, and, since we weren't rich, my assumption was that foreign travel was not for me. Later in my life two circumstances made that assumption wrong.

First, travel by airplane became much cheaper. Since the time when I was a child, the price of plane fare compared with a week's wage has dropped several fold. But something else also changed. In becoming a scientist I developed some skills and some areas of understanding that were of enough interest to others that they were willing to provide me with tickets to places scattered all over the world. This is a reflection of the fact that science is an international activity. In basic research one's colleagues are the international community of scientists. The connections of the community are maintained by communication in the scientific journals, by letters and faxes, and, increasingly, by e-mail. But all of these forms of communication are greatly aided by personal, face-to-face contacts.

In 1983 I spent five months working at the Fritz Haber Institute in what was then West Berlin. The Fritz (as it is called by the irreverent) is one of a number of Max Planck Laboratories spread throughout Germany. Each one has its research specialties, and most concentrate on basic research. My main research effort in Berlin was in the laboratory of Alex Bradshaw on problems of surface science. The presence of Elmar Zeitler's electron microscopy group next door gave me the possibility of pursuing one of my side interests, examining structures that produce iridescent colors in nature, for example in beetle shells, butterfly wings, and abalone shells.

I was reminded of the international nature of science by the library at the Fritz Haber Institute. With a few exceptions the scientific journals there in my areas of interest are the same ones that I find in my library in Milwaukee. Many of the scientific textbooks, written in German, are different from the ones I know, but the collection of scientific monographs—specialized treatments of research areas—are mostly the books also available to me and my students at home. The tradition of science is international.

Personal contact is so important to the exchange of information that it is an integral part of the system of doing science. People meet at scientific conferences, or in postdoctoral affiliations, or in sabbatical leaves spent at another institution, and visits to other nearby laboratories are piggy-backed onto any of these other activities. After the personal contact has occurred, the written and e-mailed communication is much more effective than before. My connection with Polish scientists is an example of what grows from personal contact.

Recently, in response to a friend's question, I tried to count the number of countries in which I had given scientific talks. The list included twenty-one countries spread across six of the seven continents. (The continent absent from the list is not Antarctica, where I have given several talks, but Africa.) This travel to many interesting parts of the world has been a side benefit of my profession, something totally unexpected for me as a child.

So how do I trace the road from West Unity to Warsaw? The beginnings must be connected with that laboratory of colors in the back yard, or perhaps with my childhood excitement with the rainbow and with whatever combination of influences that led me to acquire the tools of the scientist. It is easier, however, to pick up the path at a much later time. In 1971-72 I spent a year in the School of Chemical Sciences at the University of East Anglia in Norwich, England. I was working with Norman Sheppard and Dave King, both chemists with whom I shared research interests.

One day a visitor from Cambridge appeared in Norman's office. She had come from the Institute of Physical Chemistry of the Polish Academy of Sciences to Cambridge and was making only a short visit to Norwich. Irmina Ratajczykowa worked in a group in Warsaw established by Professor Waclawa Palczewska who, as a young woman a generation before, worked with Professor John Linnett at Cambridge. Through that connection it was arranged that Irmina would spend several months in Professor Linnett's laboratory, learning to use some new techniques and broadening her scientific experience.

It frequently happens that arrangements for such a visit must be made so far in advance that it is impossible to predict the state of the laboratory enterprise at the time of the visit. In this case when Irmina arrived in Cambridge, the apparatus that she was to use was not available. To solve this problem, Professor Linnet suggested that she spend some time with his friend Norman Sheppard in Norwich, learning about the use of infrared spectroscopy to study the structure of molecules that were stuck (adsorbed) onto surfaces—a subject of considerable interest in her group in Warsaw.

I met her when she arrived and talked with her for most of the afternoon. The conversation gradually slowed down until we discovered the appropriate speed for communication with her less-than-perfect facility in English and my lack of any facility in Polish. It slowly became clear that she had read—and read very carefully—all of my published papers on a new method of studying the structure of molecules adsorbed onto an extended metal surface. We discussed the method at some length.

To make the following story more understandable, perhaps I should take the time to discuss two similar words that I must use to tell it. This process of a molecule sticking to the surface of a solid material is called *adsorption* and the similarities of the word to the more familiar one, *absorption*, is the source of endless confusion with typists and proof-readers. I need to reassure you that I am really using two different words—which have three different meanings.

The more familiar word *absorption* is one that I use to describe two different processes, both of which I mention repeatedly. I talk about light being absorbed by a material. Your word intuition is probably accurate here. Some of the light that strikes a material may disappear; it is not reflected or transmitted or scattered but is swallowed up by the material and disappears: it is *absorbed*. Another process described by the same word is one in which gas molecules become attached to a solid. For example, a container of baking soda in your refrigerator may *absorb* the odor of onions stored nearby. But the process of *absorption* is one in which the gas molecules move into the *inside* of the solid material. The similar process of *adsorption* is one where the gas molecules become attached only to the *surface* of the solid material. The distinction may seem to be a picky one, but it is very important in understanding a number of processes that take place at surfaces.

In the method Irmina and I discussed on that day in Norwich, a beam of infrared light is reflected from the metal surface, at the appropriate angle, into an infrared spectrometer that analyzes the light. We find narrow regions missing from the infrared spectrum, indicating that energy has been absorbed by the molecules on the surface. The frequency of the missing light matches the frequency of the natural vibrations of the adsorbed molecules, and with that, and some other information, we can deduce the structure of the molecules sitting on the surface.

One expects such information to be useful in understanding how a catalyst works in a situation where, for example, two molecules will not react to form some desired product until one, or perhaps both of them, adsorb on the metal surface. The process of adsorption changes the molecule(s) enough that the reaction takes place and the newly formed molecules resulting from the reaction depart the surface, leaving it ready to repeat the process with another set of molecules. The metal surface is acting as the catalyst for the chemical reaction. It seemed obvious to me that the key step to understanding how the catalyst works must lie in understanding the changes that take place in the molecule when it is adsorbed. My infrared technique showed promise of giving information about those changes.

The name of Irmina's group in Warsaw was Catalysis on Metals, and she had wanted to introduce this technique into her laboratory. It was a surprise to her to find one of the originators of the method working in Norwich. One result of this chain of chance events is that Irmina rearranged her stay in England to spend most of her time in Norwich to become proficient in the technique, which she then introduced into her laboratory at home. Later, when I first met John Linnett at a meeting, I introduced myself by telling him that I came forward to admit having perpetrated a larceny against him. In responding to his surprised reaction, I identified Irmina's research efforts as the thing I had stolen from his laboratory. He reassured me that it had worked out very well for her to work in Norwich, and he was pleased that the arrangement provided a good experience for her while she was in England.

As a result of this collaboration I was invited later in the year to be part of a conference arranged in Warsaw by Irmina's institute at the Polish Academy of Sciences. Of the one hundred scientists attending, roughly half were from Poland, a quarter from Western Europe, and a quarter from other Eastern European countries. I was the singularity, the only person from outside Europe. It was interesting at that conference to see scientists from East and West Germany, working in the same field, meet for the first time. Although they may have read one another's papers, the politics of the time did not allow visits to the other's country; however, the politics did allow them to go to Poland.

What started as a chance encounter in Norwich developed into a cooperative arrangement that resulted in ten visits to Poland over the next twenty years. In addition, four people from Warsaw spent time working in my institution. Several of these visits were financed by a grant through the National Science Foundation using "special foreign currency funds." This was money owed the United States for various assistance projects in countries where the currency was not convertible on the world market. Some of these funds were made available to support cooperative scientific research programs. Later the Optical Society of America helped support some visits to the optical science community. The story of a scientific collaboration is also the story of personal friendships.

On one of my early visits to Poland I was taken to dinner by three friends, Irmina, Irena, and Ryszard, and was led to understand that they had something very important to discuss with me. "Which organization," they asked me, "do you think is the most powerful organization in Poland?"

It seemed to be a very serious question, and my reply was cautious. "Is it the Communist Party?"

"Perhaps not the Communist Party," I was told, "but perhaps an organization known as the ZZS."

I was told that the ZZS was much more exclusive, and the source of its power was that its members could "give the pin" to anybody. I found out that ZZS stands for Zwiazek Zbieraczy Szpilek, which translates as Society of Pin Collectors. The meaning of "giving someone the pin" turns out to translate rather well into the English idiom of "needling" someone. The prime requisite for membership in ZZS was that not only did a person need to be skilled in giving the pin, but he or she needed to be able to smile when being given the pin. The membership had decided that I qualified—on both scores—and was to be inducted as the first foreign member of this exclusive society. In fact, the society was so exclusive that the entire membership was attending this dinner!

I decided that my usual objection to secret societies did not apply to the ZZS. Later we expanded the group to include others, including members from England and Germany. Meetings were held whenever three or more members got together at some scientific gathering, and the agenda consisted of having dinner and perhaps passing a resolution condemning the leadership of the organization and suggesting that it was time to throw the rascal out—and elect a new president. The "meetings" continued through the time of the Solidarity movement in Poland, and photographs were taken of the members in front of Solidarity banners. After that the political mood of the country changed to the point that I, as sometime president of this group, no longer felt comfortable in sending photos and mock resolutions through the mail to my friends in Poland. Political systems are not known to have well-developed senses of humor.

In the early 1970s my wife, Barbara, accompanied me on a visit to Warsaw, and our friends arranged an elegant meal for us in the wine cellar of an old palace outside the city. It was the kind of elegance that disappeared from the public scene shortly after that time. The entree was venison, and the meal consisted of many courses. I think I never have been confronted with a more extensive array of stemware and silverware surrounding the plate. Of course, the thing that really made it so special, and memorable to this day, was the presence of good friends.

At that time we were trying to arrange for one of the people, Ryszard Dus, to spend some months at my lab in Milwaukee. During the meal, surrounded by the candles and glittering glassware, I said, "Ah, Ryszard, this is indeed splendid, but if you do come to Milwaukee I will take you to a restaurant known as McDonald's!" Said Ryszard, "This McDonald's must be a wonderful place." (At that time the McDonald's chain was not well-known in Europe.) "No matter," said I. "If you come, I *promise* to take you there!" Ryszard did come to Milwaukee and, true to my word, I did arrange a meal at McDonald's with him. And, true to the spirit of the ZZS, Ryszard pronounced it a wonderful place, coming up with the slogan, "A Day Without McDonald's is a Day Wasted."

Even the official channels of the Polish government became involved with our McDonald's game. Shortly before Ryszard was to depart Warsaw for Milwaukee, I sent him a brief, hand-written note saying that I would meet him when his plane arrived at the airport and that I had not forgotten my promise to take him to McDonald's. When getting permission to leave the country, which was a necessary step in getting his passport, he found that he needed to have an official letter of invitation from me, which he did not have, so he brought this note to serve that purpose. Later he described the disdain with which the official read and reread the note, sighed mightily, and, finally, as he decided to sign the necessary documents, said with obvious restraint, "You might tell Professor Greenler that, in the future, it would be appreciated if he were a little less informal in these matters."

> So as I swing down the street in Warsaw, my mood is influenced by the magic of an early spring day—with newly flowering spring bulbs and fruit trees smothered by heavy blankets of blossoms—and my sense of being in a place where I have good friends. All of a sudden I am struck with the strangeness of my being in this place that is so distant from West Unity. And as I think about it, I am impressed that the most remarkable thing about the experience is that, for whatever combination of reasons, it really doesn't feel strange at all.

Chapter Four

THE SOUTH POLE

The air glitters and sparkles. Tiny flashes of light appear at arm's length, in front of my face, all around me. A brilliant sun illuminates the flat, white plain that meets the sky along a distant line—broken only by the contour of the large geodesic dome and the few other buildings that constitute the United States Scott-Amundsen research station at the South Pole.

Dominating this Antarctic scene is a large halo of light circling the sun, embellished on either side by brilliant, red-edged sun dogs. An up-curving arc touches the halo at the top. A line of light parallel to the horizon is etched around the entire sky, passing through the sun dogs and the sun. The jewel in this crown of light is a brilliant, rainbow-hued arc high above the sun. I know this arc from milder climes. It lies on a circle centered on the zenith point, directly over my head, and takes its name from its place in the sky: the circumzenithal arc.

I know that all of these effects result from sunlight refracted and reflected by tiny ice crystals falling through the cold air, but I see immediately that there are at least two different groups of ice crystals involved. The circumzenithal arc and sun dogs are all smoothly painted with brilliant light, and they have a different texture from the arc at the top of the halo. That arc is not a continuous blend of colors but appears to be made up of many discrete points of light. Each point of light comes from an individual ice crystal close to me in the air. The entire arc at the top of the halo must be produced by sunlight refracted by the tiny ice crystals that are glittering close around me. Now I see why they have been referred to as "diamond dust." Those other smoothly painted arcs are clearly coming from a set of ice crystals higher in the sky, far enough from me that I do not see spots of light from individual crystals. Instead, I see the beautiful, smooth pattern produced by the millions of ice crystals falling slowly through the sun-lit sky, directing light to my eager eye. This is what I have come to the end of the earth to study—and the beauty and excitement of the display make me want to run and dance and shout under the Antarctic sun.

Such an intense feeling, one that calls for some physical expression, brings to my mind the delight of a small boy, excited by the magic of a rainbow appearing in the sky following the passage of a summer thunderstorm. The connection between that boy and his adult, standing at the South Pole forty years later, may be a twisty, meandering path, traveled without conscious intent, but it represents a continuity in my life. What are some of the markers along this path?

The rainbow remained a part of my life, a part of the world that gave me pleasure, but not a conscious part of the process that led me to become a scientist. When I was a graduate student in the 1950s, a book helped point me along the path that led, among other places, to the South Pole. Dover Publishers reissued an out-of-print volume, *The Nature of Light and Colour in the Open Air,* by Dutch astronomer Marcel Minnaert. It became a significant book for me.

Minnaert describes a wide collection of optical phenomena in the world around us that can be observed with the naked eye. He includes the effects of light and shadow, of the refraction and reflection of light, of mirages, and of the wide variety of optical effects caused by light scattering and the interaction of light with ice crystals and water droplets. The theme of the book is described by the author in his preface to the original edition: "The phenomena described in this book are partly things you can

Chapter Four:
THE SOUTH POLE

The rainbow that started the trail to the South Pole.

(All photos by author unless noted)

The sun pillar and upper tangent both result from the same set of airborne ice crystals. This is the photo used on the cover of the May-June 1972 issue of *American Scientist* that carried our first article on sun pillars.

(Photo by A. James Mallmann)

A glitter path on water results from a process very similar to that which produces a sun pillar.

The entrance to the dome at the South Pole when I first arrived in January 1977.

The ceremonial South Pole marker, surrounded by the national flags of the original signers of the Antarctic Treaty. The geodesic dome can be seen in the distance.

The author and "R2D2" at the South Pole on a sunny summer day in January 1998.

A twenty-two-degree halo at the South Pole.

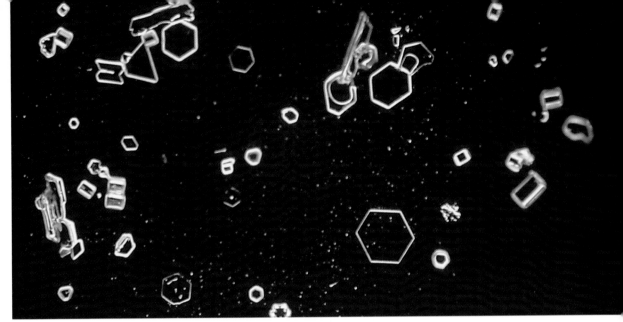

Microscopic view of tiny "diamond dust" ice crystals that produce spectacular halos in Antarctica. The biggest crystal in the photograph is about a third of a millimeter in diameter.

A South Pole display showing several beautiful halo effects.

A white rainbow at the South Pole, resulting from very small, supercooled water droplets.

Chapter Six: *THE SCIENCE BAG*

From a 1974 *Science Bag* program, "Whiter than White, Blacker than Black,
and Greener than Green: The Perception of Color."
(Science Bag *photos by Alan Magayne-Roshak*)

The 1984 program, "The Clarinet, The Washtub and the Musical Nails: How Musical Instruments Work."

A 1995 program, "Glowing Eyes and Personal Halos: Seeing the Light."

***Chapter Seven*: MICHAEL FARADAY AND THE ROYAL INSTITUTION**

Barbara and Robert, just before the Friday Evening Discourse.
(Photo by Raymond F. Newell, Jr.)

The painting, now hanging in Faraday's office, titled,
[   ] *WHO ACCIDENTALLY SAID "LADIES AND GENTLEMEN" AT THE RI*

(Photo by Raymond F. Newell, Jr.)

observe in everyday life, and partly things as yet unfamiliar to you, though they may be seen at any moment if only you will touch your eyes with that magic wand called 'knowing what to look for.' And then there are those rare, remarkable wonders of nature that happen only once in a lifetime, so that even trained observers may wait year after year to see them. When they do see them, they are filled with a sense of extraordinary happiness."

Two things about the book, in addition to the subject matter, greatly impressed me. One is Minnaert's urging us to look at the world in a way to see what is really there. This is what Quaker artist Sylvia Shaw Judson describes in her introduction to *The Quiet Eye: A Way of Looking at Pictures* as "looking with fresh eyes." I believe that our normal condition is that of being blind, even to obvious things around us, if someone has not drawn our attention to them. I remember when I became interested in identifying mushrooms and found that suddenly the world was filled with brilliantly colored mushrooms that one could hardly help noticing but that, to my awareness, had never been there before. I had started to look at another part of the world with fresh eyes. Minnaert urges us to look and try to see what is there. Over a period of several years Dover issued the reprint of his book with three different covers. Ironically, the last cover shows a stylized rainbow with colors in the wrong order. The people involved in producing the cover had not learned one of Minnaert's lessons.

The second lesson I learned from this book has to do with a style of writing. I was greatly impressed with someone who would write, "A bright ring with a radius of rather more than 22° can be seen surrounding the sun; the best way to see it is to stand in the shade of a house or to hold your hand against the sun to prevent yourself from being dazzled. It is a grand sight!" Or who, after describing the possible explanations for sun pillars, would end with, "The pillars of light seemed such a simple phenomenon. Who would have thought that their explanation would incur so many difficulties?"

I realized that revealing the personal involvement of the scientist with his or her work—or commenting on the beauty of the effects being studied—in no way detracts from the science being discussed. That book *was*, and *is*, for me a lesson in how science can be humanized by our willingness to show the enthusiasm and the aesthetic involvement that is a part of our work. Minnaert's example launched my small, life long campaign to loosen up the scientific literature by writing in the first-person active voice, rather than the third-person passive, and letting some of the personal motivation and involvement with the research show in the reporting.

I came to another turning point on that meandering path to the South Pole not long after I became a faculty member. I was talking one afternoon in 1966 to an undergraduate student, George Blumenthal. I don't think that George was a student in any of my classes, and I don't know how we got talking about sun pillars, but we did. A sun pillar is a vertical streak of light, either above or below the sun, usually seen when the sun is low in the sky. It results from sunlight that is reflected off the surface of minute ice crystals slowly falling through the air.

It is a familiar experience to most of us involved in research that we sometimes get new insight into our work when we try to explain it to an intelligent listener. If a person has the background to understand what we are doing but is not familiar with the details of the project, we are led to explain things in a way that brings our unconscious assumptions and conclusions into the light for a fresh examination. Sometimes that process of explaining will bring new insight, even without any direct participation from the listener. Even so, the presence of the intelligent listener is crucial, because without his or her presence, it is too easy to slip over some link in the chain of reasoning without examining it. Of course, the listener's questions or suggestions are frequently fruitful in the discussion as well. This kind of face-to-face conversation is so valuable in the doing of science that even the modern array of electronic communications cannot replace it.

George was an intelligent and interested listener, so I was motivated to give him a detailed description of how sun pillars are produced and why they have the form they do. As my description became more careful, the conversation slowed until the explanation ground to a halt as I realized that I myself didn't understand how sun pillars are produced. For a decade I thought I understood sun pillars, but until I tried to explain them to George, I didn't know that I didn't know. As we continued our discussion, we began to realize that the conventional explanation didn't describe the shape of some sun pillars and that perhaps other people also didn't understand their formation.

The usual explanation attributed these pillars to the reflection of light from the flat faces of hexagonal, plate-shaped ice crystals. As such crystals fall through the air, they tend to orient so that their flat faces are horizontal—the same orientation as that taken by a falling leaf or by a sky diver falling through the air with outstretched arms and legs. Sunlight can be reflected to your eye from the nearly horizontal bottom surfaces of those ice crystals that are located in the atmosphere above your line of sight to the sun. Such rays produce a column of light extending above the sun. Those crystals located below your sun line of sight will reflect sunlight to produce a column of light below the sun. A perfect analogy for the reflection from those lower crystals is the "glitter path" of sunlight reflected from the surface of slightly rough water. Although little elements of the water surface may be tilted in any direction from the horizontal, the reflected light takes the form of a vertical streak.

This explanation seemed adequate to explain some observed sun pillars but not others. For example, sometimes, when the sun is fairly high in the sky, the pillars appear as short, vertical columns centered on the sun, extending both above and below. It seemed that we could not understand those pillars from the usual explanation.

George and I ended that conversation by talking about how we could use the computer to reproduce the appearance of the sun pillars if, indeed, they were produced by the usually assumed mechanism. We could use the computer to trace light rays reflected off an array of little surfaces, each tilted slightly from the horizontal, and plot a dot to mark the position of each crystal reflecting light to the observer's eye. The reflections from ten thousand little ice crystals would produce a pattern composed of ten thousand dots on the paper, the pattern showing the form of the sun pillar resulting from those crystal reflections. Such a simulation would clearly show the light pattern we would expect to see from a collection of ice crystals with the tilt angles we had chosen. We saw that we could start with a suggestion of how a sun pillar is produced and then do the computer simulation to display the form of the pillar that would result from that suggestion. If the simulation matched the appearance of the observed pillar, the suggestion would probably be correct.

George started the calculations, but long before we had finished the project, he graduated and went on to graduate school, on his way to becoming an astrophysicist.

Progress on the project was slow. I was trying to organize my research program (in a different area from this little diversion), help develop a research-oriented physics department, and help establish an interdisciplinary Laboratory for Surface Studies. I also found myself serving on many of the major committees of a university in the process of changing from an undergraduate teaching campus to a graduate, research-oriented institution. There were many things to do.

Two years after we began these sun-pillar simulations, Professor Minnaert was giving an invited talk at the annual meeting of the Optical Society of America, held that year in Detroit. I was eager to be a part of the session featuring this man, whom I felt I knew from his writing, and I submitted an abstract for a paper giving our preliminary sun-pillar results. It was a pleasure to meet Minnaert, seventy-four years old at that time, who turned out to be as friendly a person as I had imagined. We agreed that I had not yet solved the sun-pillar puzzle but that I had a promising start.

The morning after our session Minnaert spotted me in the lobby of the conference hotel as he came down for breakfast. He came over to me and exclaimed with great enthusiasm, "Ahh, last night I had the most marvelous dream; I dreamed about your *wonderful* sun pillars!" And thus does one generation inspire the next.

Six years after that first conversation with George we finally published a paper about sun pillars in *American Scientist*, with a color photo on the cover. The photo shows a pillar rising above the setting sun, surmounted by a dramatic, V-shaped arc. A former graduate student, Jim Mallmann, who as a student had worked with me on a problem unrelated to sky effects, got involved with this project, starting a productive cooperation that lasted for more than a decade and resulted in the joint authorship of nine papers. Jim's very significant contribution to the sun-pillar puzzle was the computer program he wrote, enabling us to trace the paths of sunlight rays that pass *through* the crystal. Such rays are refracted at each surface and so are deviated from their original directions, as happens when light rays are deviated in their passage through the more familiar glass prism.

Our conclusion in the *American Scientist* paper is that sun pillars are produced by two different mechanisms. Our computer simulations show that reflections from the nearly horizontal faces of flat-plate crystals do produce pillars, as had been previously assumed, but there is an addditional mechanism. Another small ice-crystal form known to exist in the atmosphere is that of a hexagonal column. I call it a pencil crystal because of its similarity to the shape of a wooden pencil before it is sharpened. Think of the lead in the pencil as the crystal axis. Such a crystal, in the appropriate size range, will tend to fall with its axis horizontal. You can see the effect by throwing a handful of grass blades in the air and seeing how they fall.

It came as something of a surprise, then, to find that a distribution of such pencil crystals, with horizontal axes but with those axes pointing in any direction of the compass, and with random rotations of the crystals about their axes, could also produce sun pillars. Although sunlight reflected from the surfaces of such a distribution of pencil crystals could bring light to an observer's eye from any place in the sky, there is a concentration of this reflected light that forms a vertical column of light, extending through the sun. The evidence that really convinced us, and others, of these explanations came from two photographs of nature's own sun pillars.

In addition to the pillar produced by reflected light, each of these photos shows another effect resulting from light refracted as it passes through the same crystals.

In one of these photos the shape of the pillar is matched by our simulations using light rays reflected from the flat surfaces of a flock of plate crystals with their large faces tilted by various angles from the horizontal. This was the commonly accepted explanation for the origin of sun pillars. To the side of the sun in this photo is a vertically elongated sun dog located twenty-two degrees away from the sun. This effect is matched by the simulation using rays that pass *through* the same flock of plate crystals that produce the pillar.

The other photo shows a sun pillar that is matched by our simulation using light rays reflected from the surfaces of oriented pencil crystals. In the same photo there is a V-shaped arc in the sky above the pillar. It is significant that this arc is well matched by our simulation using the rays of light that pass through the same group of ice crystals.

In each case the light rays that pass through the crystals produce distinctive arcs that tell us what kind of crystals are present in the sky, producing the sun pillar. It is symbolic of our mutual effort that one of the photos was taken by Jim and the other by me.

I was becoming more and more involved with optical sky effects, and in looking back I see that it was this involvement that made it possible for me, many years later, to stand on the Polar ice cap and view the incredible beauty of a halo display over the South Pole.

The process of looking at the big picture of optical sky phenomena was further stimulated by an invitation to talk about my interest in sky effects to a regional group of college science teachers. A colleague was organizing a weekend workshop as part of a program supported by a National Science Foundation grant. I was scheduled with these teachers for a Friday evening session and two Saturday morning sessions, each lasting between one and one-and-a-half hours. With this amount of time to use, I sat down to organize all of the material I had accumulated and to formulate explanations of the effects that I had captured in photos. I was surprised at what I learned as I did so. I began to realize that many of these effects were not very well understood!

The explanation of the rainbow was in pretty good shape. In the early 1600s French philosopher and mathematician René Descartes had mathematically traced a series of rays of sunlight through water drops. He identified the bright primary bow as resulting from rays that entered the drop and then traveled to the other side of the drop, where some were reflected back to exit on the side they entered. For such rays to come to the eye of an observer, the individual must stand looking away from the sun and see the rainbow on the other side of the sky. Using the law of refraction and the index of refraction of water, Descartes was able to predict from his model the location, shape, and size of the primary rainbow. Further, by considering rays that made two internal reflections in the water drop before exiting, he correctly placed the fainter, secondary bow in the sky just outside the primary bow. His explanation clearly got to the mechanism of the rainbow, but it didn't explain everything. It must have been a source of great frustration to Descartes to be able to understand so much about the rainbow but not to be able to understand the colors!

A few years later Isaac Newton in England, apparently preceded by Francesco Maria Grimaldi in Italy, understood that white light is a mixture of all of the spectral colors and that different colors are bent (refracted) by different amounts when they cross the boundary between air and water. As a result, each color appears as a slightly different-sized circle in the sky, giving the spread of rainbow colors.

Other features of the rainbow display were still unexplained in Newton's time. Sometimes, just inside the primary bow, we can see one or more fringes of light. To me they usually look like a part of the bow, with the color of the bands varying from green to pink or magenta. These fringes go by the interesting name of supernumerary bows. Their explanation had to await the development of the wave theory of light and the concept of interference.

In the time since I prepared that first workshop, there have been new explanations for visible features of the rainbow and new mathematical models that describe subtle features in more detail. In fact, since then I have had the great pleasure of predicting and demonstrating the existence of an invisible rainbow in the sky, not previously detected. However, in that workshop I was able to show a number of rainbow photos and give understandable explanations for a number of the features that could be seen: two bows and their shapes and colors, the greater sky brightness almost always observable inside the primary bow, and the supernumerary bows sometimes showing inside that bow.

I could also make sense out of a number of beautiful effects that arise from light scattering in the atmosphere and could come up with colorful demonstrations to capture the essence of blue sky, white clouds, and red sunsets. But when I came to sky effects resulting from the interaction of sunlight with airborne ice crystals, I found quite a different state of affairs.

The origins of science, called Natural Philosophy in the past century, are rooted in people's attempts to explain the things they observe in the world around them. Beautiful optical sky effects have always commanded people's attention, and many of the famous scientists of the eighteenth and nineteenth centuries pondered the origin of the rainbow. At the beginning of the twentieth century physicists got caught up in the new quantum physics, with the uncertainty principle, with the wave nature of matter and the particle nature of light, and with the quantization effects that underlie much of physics. During World War II physicists were drawn into matters intimately connected with new methods of defense and offense, and by the time the war was over, physics was seen by the pub-lic—and by physicists—as pretty serious stuff.

During this time investigation of certain areas went out of fashion, and this was true of investigations of beautiful sky effects. To be sure, there was an occasional paper published on sky phenomena by a scientist who had made his reputation elsewhere, but along with increasing govern-mental support for scientific research came assumptions about what constitutes "serious science."

When I was talking with Cambridge University Press in the late 1970s about writing a book on optical effects in the atmosphere, they said they were the appropriate publisher for such a book. In business for 450 years, they had a long tradition of publishing science books written for the public by prestigious scientists—Jeans, Eddington, Gamow. But, an editor told me, in this century and particularly since World War II, such scientists had become preoccupied with other things and had seldom written books for nonscientists. At a recent policy meeting Cambridge University Press had decided to make an effort to revitalize this tradition and again publish sci-ence books for the public, written by "serious" scientists. So by the time I was ready to publish a book on optical sky phenomena, there was a recognition at Cambridge that it was time to return to some of these topics that had largely disappeared from the publishing scene.

A decade earlier, when I looked for explanations of a wide variety of halos, arcs, crosses, and spots that clearly resulted from atmospheric ice crystals, I found incomplete explanations, proposed fifty years earlier and not seriously considered since. There were "shoulder-shrugging" suggestions that a particular arc probably resulted from light that entered such-and-such a crystal through this face and exited through some other face, but with no testing of the suggestion. What started for me as an attempt to look in the scientific literature for explanations of effects I had photographed, or seen, or heard of from others took on a new feel. Here was an area where many things were not understood, and our computer-simulation method was just the technique to investigate them. Progress on the explanations involved the efforts of at least a dozen people.

The computer methods for doing these simulations were worked on by a series of undergraduate students over a period of several years. The "research lifetime" of undergraduate students is rather short. There is a brief period—after they acquire enough background to work on such a project and before they graduate—in which they have a chance to contribute some new understanding. Some students never quite got up to the point of accomplishment of their predecessors. Others made it to the frontier, poised for the leap into the unknown, before their time ran out. And some would surmount the barrier and help to understand things that no one had understood before. That can be a pretty heady experience for undergraduate students, or for anyone, and their accomplishments are acknowledged by their names as coauthors on a number of papers published in the scientific journals.

Actually, I believe that the research experience can be an exciting part of students' educations, even when they don't manage to push forward the frontiers of knowledge. For most it is the first time they have ever worked on a problem where the answer is not in the back of the book (or in the instructor's manual) and where "even the professor" doesn't know the answer. There is an excitement in such a circumstance that can push back a person's horizon and give a glimpse of possibilities not previously perceived.

An interesting application of our developing expertise with computer simulations was to use the simulations to study old, published drawings of sky displays for which there were no photographs. As an example, I show here a drawing published in 1821 by W. E. Parry from his Arctic explorations. For comparison, I show our computer simulation of the effects represented in the drawing, and also a photo taken some years later at the other end of the earth. The congruence of the effects in these three figures suggests that we have developed a good understanding of the processes that produce them.

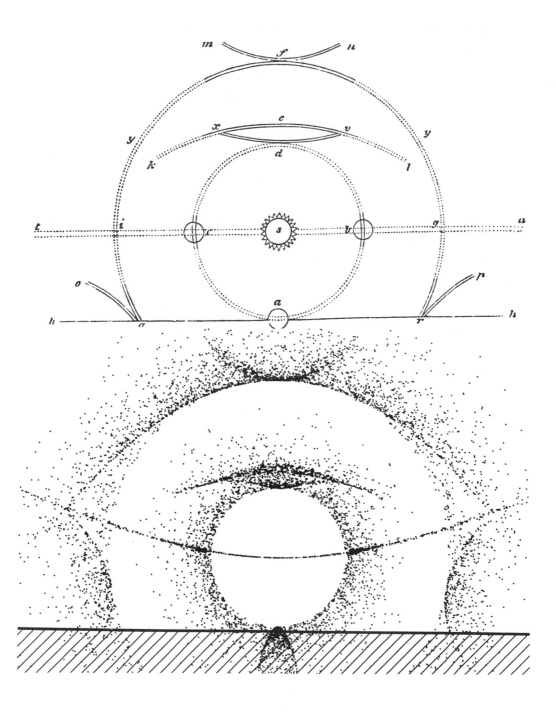

Left top: A drawing published by W.E. Parry in his book, *Journal of a Voyage for the Discovery of a Northeast Passage,* in 1821. The small arc labeled c takes its name, the Parry Arc, from this report.

Left bottom: Our computer simulation of Parry's drawing. (For a more complete discussion see Greenler's *Rainbows, Halos, and Glories*.)

Above: A South Pole photograph showing most of the features of the simulation and of Parry's drawing.

My students and colleagues and I published papers sharing the insights of our investigations into the mysteries of ice-crystal halos, and I gave talks to a variety of groups of scientists and nonscientists who seemed to be equally fascinated by these beautiful things that they could see—and understand. On some occasions, after a talk, a person would tell me that he had spent some time in Antarctica and had seen an effect that he did not understand. And I got letters from people who had read my papers, asking questions about things they had observed, sometimes with a photograph. I gradually became aware that some of the reports from Antarctica held tantalizing suggestions of sky displays that had neither been documented nor understood.

I began to ask the question of how a person might arrange to get dropped off in Antarctica for a period of time—*and then get picked up again later!* The answer lay in the provisions of the Antarctic Treaty, then signed by the twelve nations with an active interest in exploring Antarctica. These nations agreed that this southernmost continent is to be used only for peaceful purposes and activities that preserve and protect its environment. It is not to be a site for military maneuvers, waste disposal, or commercial exploitation. Permitted activity is essentially limited to exploration and scientific investigations.

In the United States this treaty led to giving the National Science Foundation (NSF) oversight of all U.S. activities in Antarctica. Although military activity in Antarctica is prohibited by the treaty agreement, it was specifically agreed that military transport could be used in the explorations. So two Coast Guard icebreakers labor their way, once a year, to McMurdo, the largest base on the coast, escorting a ship with fuel and bulky supplies for all bases. Air Force cargo planes fly from Christchurch, New Zealand, to McMurdo, and Navy aircraft provide access to research stations inland. NSF control of the activity was made very clear, however, by putting the money to support these operations in the budget of the NSF Division of Polar Programs, from whence it is dispersed to hire the Air Force, Navy, and Coast Guard to provide these services.

For me, then, the next step in that long, twisty path to Antarctica was making a research proposal to NSF. The proposal would be screened and peer-reviewed like a proposal to any other granting agency, and a successful outcome would result in a trip to this most inaccessible of continents. The proposal did turn out to be successful, and it set in motion the chain of events that finally took me to the South Pole.

The first link in this chain was an orientation session in Arizona, at that time required of all people heading for Antarctica. The orientation included information on transportation, food, clothing, housing, research facilities, and, especially, on cold-weather hazards and safety procedures. While gathering in the hot summer of Arizona, we were acquainted with the danger of being caught, even a few hundred feet from base, in a whiteout, where all traces of horizon, sky, and snow structure dissolve into a featureless white, leaving not only no visual clue to the direction of the base but also no clues to the direction of up or down. The resulting disorientation is reported to be so profound that some people are unable even to remain standing.

A physician with experience in cold-weather medical problems, acquired mostly at military bases in the Arctic, gave descriptions of cold-weather hazards, which he illustrated with stories designed for maximum impact on his listeners. He described the problem of activities, routine at familiar temperatures, that become hazardous at low-enough temperature. For example, spilling a bit of gasoline on your hand while fueling a generator at normal temperatures is no problem. At forty degrees below zero, however, gasoline may look the same, but it instantly freezes the skin that it contacts. He emphasized this cold-liquid hazard by relating the experience of a person on a military base in the Arctic who had gone to some evening entertainment away from his living quarters. He went out in the minus-forty-degree night to start his truck engine before it cooled off completely. After the cab had warmed up, before he returned to the party, he remembered the bottle of whiskey stashed under the seat and decided to have a swig of it. The physician telling us the story said, "At forty below, whiskey doesn't freeze, but a slug of whiskey at that temperature instantly freezes his gut and, since we have no way to do a gut transplant, he dies." Somehow that warning about handling liquids at low temperatures stayed with me.

In January 1977 I and others headed for Antarctica got into a big, windowless, Air Force cargo plane in California and, after being shaken about for twenty-four hours, stepped out in New Zealand in the middle of summer. Fueling stops in the darkness of Hawaii and Samoa had not added any sense of reality to this unlikely transition. In Christchurch we were issued extreme-cold-weather clothing and told to report at seven o'clock in the morning, bundled into that clothing, with all of our equipment, for the eight-hour flight to McMurdo. The next morning, after we were organized to go, the last minute weather reports from McMurdo were not good, and we were told, "Not today. Report at seven tomorrow morning."

After several days we did take off from New Zealand. Prior to our departure I made a request to go onto the flight deck during the trip and, in fact, spent most of the time standing on the flight deck where I could see the sky and the collage of sea ice and icebergs in the waters surrounding the continent. Approaching McMurdo, we flew for nearly one thousand miles along the spectacular Transantarctic Mountain Range, looking down on snow, ice, rock, mountains, and glacier-filled valleys.

I was reminded of a childhood fantasy. When I scrambled down a steep slope or clambered over a rock to get at some isolated spot, I sometimes wondered, just before I put my foot in some particular, inaccessible niche, if anyone on this earth had ever before set a foot right THERE. As I viewed this spectacular Antarctic snowscape, that fantasy returned. I had a vision of what this continent would look like if everyone who ever walked on it had left blue footprints. Around the bases on the coast and around the research stations inland the land/ice would be solid blue, completely covered with overlapping tracks. But the solid color would be gone a few miles away. Isolated tracks would crisscross the continent, but large, large areas of that inaccessible terrain would show not a single, blue footprint.

I spent a day at McMurdo and then left on an LC130 plane that took off, on wheels from a sea-ice runway, on the 800-mile trip to the South Pole. We followed the edge of the Ross ice shelf, where we could see snapshot views of the glaciers pouring through gaps in the Transantarctic Mountains down to the sea. Then we rose up over the mountains to the high, featureless polar plateau that extends for hundreds of miles, covering central Antarctica. Finally, we could make out the distant profiles of the geodesic dome and the few buildings that formed the Scott-Amundsen research station. As we neared the station, it appeared to be a fragile human habitat, a slight interruption to the empty whiteness of the Antarctic plain. The plane landed on the snow strip on skis with the wheels retracted. We had arrived at the bottom of the earth.

I was not disappointed in what I found in the Antarctic skies. Of course, one always wants to see more, and surely there is always more to see. When I got up from sleeping, I would take a look at the sky before breakfast. The sun would be about twenty degrees above the horizon. Six hours later, after lunch, the sun would still be about twenty degrees above the horizon, as it would be after dinner and when I would get up to check the sky in the middle of my sleeping time.

Although we call the time after sleeping "morning," it is an entirely arbitrary designation based on our experiences in other parts of the world. At the pole, with twenty-four consecutive hours of daylight in the Antarctic summertime, there is nothing to suggest morning, afternoon, evening, or night. As a convenience, we adopt the same time as Christchurch, since that is our logistical connection with the rest of the world.

When I was anticipating the Antarctic trip, people with whom I discussed it tended to divide into two groups. One reaction was, "Why would anyone want to go to such a godforsaken place?" The other was, "Don't you need someone to carry your suitcase?" While I was there, I never got over the wonder of being at that unique place on this globe where, all day long, the sun circles the sky at constant elevation above a horizon that lies, everywhere, to the north.

> I am surrounded by sparkling diamond dust and a slowly changing display of brilliant halos, arcs, spots, and streaks projected onto the blue dome of my sky. With significant effort I concentrate on getting photographs with the right exposures and with the right lenses, on collecting the falling ice crystals and preserving them for later photography, and on recording the relevant data before these wondrous manifestations fade. All the time the exhilaration of the small boy watching the rainbow bubbles just below the surface.

The restrictions of a teaching schedule made that a short trip; I spent only about three weeks in Antarctica and only two weeks at the Pole. The second year of the NSF grant supported a field trip to Point Barrow, at the northernmost projection of Alaska. I was housed at the Naval Arctic Research Station, which has since been closed. I went there in late March, and I saw and photographed some impressive ice-crystal effects that, to my knowledge, had not been photographed before. An unexpected bonus of that trip came one day when great changes appeared out over the ice-covered Arctic Ocean. Pillars and columns and walls material-ized, all part of a dramatic fata morgana mirage, which I'll discuss more in a later chapter.

Antarctica still had a strong grip on me, and I wanted to go back to the South Pole. The way to do it was to apply for another three-year grant to support continuing research on optical effects from air-borne ice crystals. To justify the support, the next proposal should expand my research in a direction that I was hesitant to go. I was trying to work this activity in with my research program on surface science and a host of other activi-ties at my home institution, and clearly more time and effort on this pro-ject would significantly affect the others. I reluctantly decided not to let my attraction to this southern place control my research priorities. Although I would continue to be involved in optical sky effects, I con-cluded that I would probably not return to the South Pole. However, I had not foreseen the consequences of my relationship with Walt Tape.

A couple of years before my first trip to Antarctica, I had given a talk at Beloit College, in southeastern Wisconsin, and there met a young mathematician named Walt Tape. He seemed to be intrigued by these ice-crystal phenomena. Later he was at the University of Wisconsin campus at Eau Claire, building a very impressive collection of sky-effect photos. One of our graduate students who came from the Eau Claire campus told of his math professor excusing himself during a lecture to step outside and take a picture during an interesting sky display. Of course, I knew that was Walt.

Walt published papers in *Scientific American* and in scientific journals, then took a leave from Eau Claire to spend a year in Fairbanks, at the University of Alaska, pursuing his interest in ice-crystal sky phenomena. He became one of the major players in the international group of scientists who study these beautiful effects. He once remarked at a scientific meeting that he had never even heard of these things until he heard Bob Greenler talk about them at Beloit College. Later, after he had moved permanently to Fairbanks and had spent a couple of field seasons in Antarctica, he told me, "You know, Bob, you really changed my life." I assume that Walt's beautiful book, *Atmospheric Halos*, has also helped change the lives of some other people.

After four seasons in Antarctica, followed by a break of six years, Walt again succumbed to the fascination of the South Polar skies and obtained support for more field work at the Pole for the 1997-98 season. He invited me to be a part of the expedition. My retirement from teaching made my absence from the University feasible, and I accepted his invitation to return to the Pole, twenty-one years after my first trip. I was at the Pole from the middle of December until they closed the station the middle of February. After a plane left the South Pole on February 16, only twenty-eight people remained. The earliest they could leave was with the next airplane flight, sometime the following October. Until that flight came, eight months later, they were THERE, dead or alive. They had made a very different commitment to Antarctica than had I.

One of my parts in the project was to set up a video camera to track the sun twenty-four hours a day and record time-lapse photos of the ice-crystal halos. We had many equipment problems and the cloudiest January on record at the Pole. Even though temperatures were in the minus twenties and minus thirties (Fahrenheit), the clouds were of super-cooled water droplets, not ice crystals. I returned the following season, in November of 1998, trying to get to the Pole as early as possible to get the equipment set up and operating.

The weather in the early part of the Antarctic spring is dicey, and it took four tries to make the jump from Christchurch to McMurdo. Two of these involved the discouraging experience of flying for ten hours in the crowded, noisy, dark, uncomfortable hold of a cargo plane before landing, back in Christchurch, after weather conditions (wind and blowing snow) had deteriorated at McMurdo to make landing there impossible.

After getting the time-lapse equipment operating, we did record some interesting displays, but not the best we expected the polar sky to yield. I turned the halo equipment over to three competent halo enthusiasts from Finland, who would operate it for the rest of the season, and I returned to Wisconsin just before Christmas. The payoff for this effort came on January 11, 1999, with a spectacular halo display, perhaps the most extensive ever recorded.

Living and working at the Pole is an intense experience, both physically and emotionally demanding. The elevation of the station is over nine thousand feet, and the temperature of the air and the circulation of the atmosphere gives an effective elevation of over ten thousand feet. Working outside and wearing heavy boots and clothing, one feels the effects of the altitude. It is somewhere between "difficult" and "impossible" to get outside help for equipment that malfunctions, so resourcefulness and ingenuity are the keys to a successful field season.

After I returned home from the last trip, I think that my dreams for the first week or two revealed something about the experience. Each night in my dreams I struggled, trying to make things work in Antarctica, trying to solve problems of equipment or logistics, trying to do things that I couldn't quite do. One night the setting of the dream was on the moon, but the situation was exactly the same, trying to make things work in a remote and harsh environment.

There is a reason why the average age of all of the participants in the U.S. Antarctic program that season was thirty-six (even after averaging in my advanced age).

I assume, as I write this book, that I have made my last trip to the end of the earth. But my Antarctic involvement has been a great experience and is only one of several unanticipated adventures that followed from my asking questions about what it is that I see in the sky.

Chapter Five

STUDENT RECOMMENDATIONS

Ron sticks his head in my office door and tells me that he has talked with the advisor at the Medical College. It appears that he will be accepted as a graduate student for the next semester in their biophysics program if he does well enough in the course he is taking there now. He has the impression that the letter I wrote helped his case. In the letter I acknowledged that Ron's academic record was mixed. After high school his poor records at a state university and a community college accurately reflected his lack of interest and sense of purpose at that time. My impression is that after working a few years, his attitude has changed, and his undergraduate record has changed with it. I ended my letter with the paragraph: "My prediction is that Ron will be a successful student and scientist. If I were making the decision about accepting him into a graduate program, I would consider him a good prospect, one whom I would expect to succeed."

I think of the chain of events, only understood some years later, that resulted in my being a graduate student in the Physics Department at Johns Hopkins University. As a third-year student at the University of Rochester I took the course in physical chemistry taught by Professor W. Albert Noyes, Jr. We students realized that he was a prominent scientist, recent president of the American Chemical Society, editor of journals, member of advisory committees and panels—a "big Noise in chemistry" we called him. I was impressed that as busy as his schedule was, he seldom missed a lecture, even though he might give a lecture after arriving in the morning from Washington and before catching a plane to New York in the evening.

Presumably because of his busy schedule, he had some help in the course from Professor A.B.F. Duncan, who gave an occasional lecture, ran the laboratory, and managed the exams. The differences in personalities between the two professors were extreme. Professor Noyes was extroversive, at home in front of a class, his lectures adorned with witty asides. Professor Duncan was shy, avoiding eye contact and apparently ill at ease with people. Which one would have a bigger influence on my life?

Although Professor Duncan had a way of looking away, or down, when talking with someone, he occasionally inserted an eye-to-eye glance into the conversation as a sort of emphasis. In the lab after the first exam, he came up to me and said, "You're the champ," and then shot me a quick glance from under his bushy eyebrows.

"What?"

"You're the champ. You did the best on the exam." (Another glance.)

I had aced the first exam and, as a result, he offered me a part-time job doing arithmetic.

For a modest hourly wage, using a Marchant mechanical calculator, I did calculations that were related to his research. I did not understand the big picture of what I was working on until a few years later, after I had taken a course in quantum mechanics, when I looked at a paper published by Professor Duncan in the *Journal of Chemical Physics.* The paper was on the electronic energy levels of sulfur hexafluoride, as determined by molecular orbital calculations, and it acknowledged the help of Robert Greenler with the calculations. It is almost impossible today to imagine doing such extensive calculations by hand. But without computers, there was no other choice.

In retrospect I see that I did make a very significant contribution to that research. I evaluated complicated algebraic terms for different numerical values of the parameters and then calculated the sums of series involving those terms. I had absolutely no understanding of the sources of those terms, but as I made tables of values, I would see patterns in the numbers. For example, the terms of a series might have alternating signs and be decreasing in size. If, in such a series, I came across a term with a sign the same as the previous term or one that was larger than the previous term, I would redo the calculations to see if I had made an error.

Frequently I would find a computational error, but if I could reproduce my result, I would call it to Professor Duncan's attention. My recollection is that in those cases he usually would find an error in the written expression. I remember thinking that he was in a precarious position if he had to rely only on me to catch such errors. On the other hand, I had no insight into the kinds of consistency checks or redundant calculations that he was making to back up my computations.

Some years later I found myself in the same situation as Professor Duncan. While working in the central research labs of Allis Chalmers (back when there was an Allis Chalmers Manufacturing Company that had a central research laboratory), I was thinking about the possibility of getting the infrared spectrum of molecules stuck on an extended metal surface by reflecting a beam of infrared radiation off the surface. The experiment would be difficult to set up and do and, to my mind, it would not be worth the investment of money and time without some quantitative indication that it might succeed. To get an idea of whether the experiment had a chance of success, I wanted to calculate the fraction of the light reflected from the metal surface (the reflectance) and then see how much that fraction would be changed by the presence of a thin layer of molecules on the surface. If the change were big enough, I could use it to detect an absorption band in the molecules. If it were too small, the experiment would fail.

With the mechanical calculators it took an hour or two to evaluate the equations to get these reflectances for one particular angle of the infrared light striking the surface. What I really wanted was to see how these values changed as the angle of the incident light was varied, because I thought that finding the optimum angle was crucial to the success of the experiment.

The laboratory employed a person just to do the calculations for people who had need of this service, and I was able to get some of her time for my project. With such a calculation, if there is even a very slight probability of making an error at any one operation, given enough operations, an error somewhere in the chain becomes likely. Every few days I would get the value for a point or two, and it was clear that they did not fall on a smooth curve as one would expect. In fact, the values were so unreliable that it was difficult to guess which points were the anomalous ones, and a recalculation of the point was likely to yield a new value no more or less believable than the first.

I had to conclude that the computing facility just could not do such a complicated calculation with a reasonable amount of effort, and I abandoned the project until a later time. I suspect that if Professor Duncan had had to rely on this computing facility for his much more complicated molecular orbital calculations, he would not have been successful. For me the reflectance problem had to wait until I went to the university and had the use of the university computer, an IBM 1620 with a memory of 20K, upgraded a few years later to 60K. But my calculations apparently helped Professor Duncan in his research and thereby also benefited me.

As I was applying to graduate schools the following year, Professor Duncan asked me about my plans. When I mentioned that Johns Hopkins University was one of the three places to which I was applying, he indicated that he knew the head of the physics department there and said, "I would be willing (glance) to write a letter of recommendation for you to Professor Dieke. In fact, (glance) I would be happy (glance) to write a letter." Of course, I accepted his offer, even though he was a chemist and I was applying to a physics department.

I received offers of teaching assistantships at two of the institutions and an offer of a Presidential Scholarship to Johns Hopkins, which helped me decide on a graduate school. I understood more about the process later when I came across a book titled, *The Spectroscopy of Uranium Compounds,* written by G. H. Dieke and A. B. F. Duncan, and I understood even more when I began to write and read student recommendations.

It's called "the old boys' network." As women become more a part of it, I assume the name will change, but the institution will remain, because it serves a useful function. It is very difficult to know what a recommendation means if you don't have the recommender calibrated. One person's glowing report of a student's abilities (either supported or contradicted by the grade transcript) may be a weaker recommendation than someone else's observation that this seems to be a rather competent student—but without knowing the people, you cannot interpret the message. The system has its problems; it tends to be exclusionary. It is easy to see its effect in any President of the United States who surrounds himself with advisors who come, too often, from his circle of former friends and associates. He is trying to deal with people whom he already has calibrated, and hence understands, from experiences less tainted with political power than the present one.

So the specific chain of events that took me to graduate school at Johns Hopkins started with my getting the best grade on the first exam in the physical chemistry course at Rochester.

> **A few moments later, as I see Ron passing my door, I call him in and say that I would like to show him the letter I wrote. Why? I think that it will be good for him to know what my expectation is for his academic performance. It might also be to his advantage to know how the recommendation system works.**

THE SCIENCE BAG

"**W**e raised three children on *The Science Bag*," says the woman as we are both leaving the lecture room after a Friday night presentation. "For years we came with them every month to the new program. It was one of our most favorite activities." Of course, I am pleased to hear her comments, even though I have heard quite a number of similar remarks over the past twenty-five years. Imagine, twenty-five years; it has been that long since Glenn Schmieg and I developed *The Science Bag* from our "what-somebody-ought-to-do" discussion.

"What somebody ought to do is present a science program on the campus on a Friday night, designed for the community, not the University. Dress it up with demonstrations to capture and keep people's interest. People come out to see shows in the planetarium, offered to the public in the evening; we could appeal to a broader group. We keep complaining about the lack of public understanding or interest in science, and this would be a way to address that problem. And the University keeps trying to sell itself to its urban neighbors by telling them of all the contributions we bring to the community. We could make an obvious and visible contribution if someone would organize a series of science programs, designed especially for the community. Somebody really ought to do that!"

The conversation stopped. Both of us realized that *nobody* will do what *somebody* ought to do—unless somebodies, like us, quit talking about it and do it. "So, shall we do it? Yeah, let's do it."

The College of Letters and Science agreed to provide a modest yearly budget so that we could offer each speaker some money for supplies, to develop demonstrations, or to hire student helpers. We named the series, *The Science Bag*, and in December 1973 I gave the first presentation titled, "Rainbows, Halos, Sun Dogs, and Other Neat Effects." From the beginning the format for the series was to have the same program repeated by the same speaker on each Friday evening of a calendar month. The following month would bring a different program and a different speaker. After some experimentation we settled on five speakers in five different months each year. Recently, in addition to the four or five Friday presentations each month, we have added one Sunday matinee. The twenty-three programs of the first year attracted 2,800 people. We had twenty-seven programs the second year with a total attendance of nearly 6,700. After some nights when people not only filled the seats but stood in the back and sat on the steps, we decided that, although that was a wonderful crowd to address, we were probably violating fire regulations and in the future should turn away overflow crowds.

Glenn and I each presented a new program every year, and we carefully recruited faculty from any of the science departments to do other programs. We insisted that no matter how good, a lecture itself wasn't good enough. The program needed to have slides, film clips, and demonstrations— which needed to be bigger than a bread box to be effective in the 250-seat lecture hall—and a variety of presentations to stretch the attention spans of the attendees. *The Science Bag* was not to be a lecture, it was to be a show. This philosophy still guides the shape of *Science Bag* programs. After nine years, Glenn moved on to other things, and I continued to run the program.

We were surprised to find that sometimes even a speaker who developed an innovative program would have no good suggestions for a title. We worked at coming up with names to catch people's attention and found that we had a group of fans who looked forward to reading the titles for each new season. The names of the 137 different programs of the first twenty-five years suggest the wide variety of presentation. They include:

- "The Clarinet, the Washtub, and the Musical Nails: How Musical Instruments Work"
- "Sugar, Quartz, and Diamonds: Crystalline Perfection"
- "Digestion: A Tough Dirty Job, It Takes a Lot of Guts"
- "The Prevailing Westerlies, the Horse Latitudes, and the Doldrums: Global Air Circulation"
- "Folding, Flooding, and Faulting: How the Earth is Shaped"
- "The Complete Pig"
- "Up Close and Personal: A View Through the World's Best Microscopes"
- "The Mirage, the Discovery of Greenland, and the Green Flash"
- "San Francisco, Charles Richter, and the Liquid Core: Our Shaking, Quaking Earth"
- "Sticks and Stones and Broken Bones: How Archeologists Work"
- "Space, Time, Einstein, and Spacetime"
- "Whiter-Than-White, Blacker-Than-Black, and Greener-Than-Green: The Perception of Color"
- "Snow White, the Flying Fox, and the Midnight Warbler: Bats of the World"
- "The Body, the Bratwurst, and the Buttress: The Strength of Structures"

There are of course, many others. People came, expecting to enjoy the presentation; they often left excited by what they had heard and seen.

Whom do we get to put in the great effort that it takes to prepare the program and then set up and perform five times over a month? When I talk to a prospective speaker, I suggest that it will take somewhere between seventy and one hundred hours to prepare and perform. When it is over, he or she will receive the use of the modest amount of left over money to support some research or scholarly activity, and a *thank you*. If these rewards are not enough to give the project sufficient priority so that it really gets the time it needs, I urge the person to turn down my invitation. Once, in the early years, when someone was concerned whether or not he had the time to do it, I urged him to give it a try. It was a mistake; he didn't have the time to do it. I vowed never to urge someone again; it would be better to cancel a month's programs.

Many of the speakers are so impressed with the amount of work it takes to put together a good program, and set up and take down for five performances, that one month's presentations are enough. Others, perhaps with poorer memories, are willing to develop another after a few years. And then there are some who finish with a sense of exhilaration and are already starting to think about the next program they would like to give.

The attitude in the University has changed over the twenty-five years since we started *The Science Bag*. A number of people in our science departments considered public education as a diversion, okay if one really liked that sort of thing, but not the job of a real scientist. The attitude toward a person who devoted a significant amount of his or her energies to such a program was viewed in different ways in different departments. In some it was considered a valued activity; in others it might be taken as an indication that the person was not a serious, totally dedicated researcher.

I made it a policy not to approach young faculty members about giving a *Science Bag* presentation until they had earned tenure. The attitude in the scientific and academic community has shifted over the past two decades, with a growing awareness of the importance of having practicing scientists talk to the public about their activities. More and more lip service is given to the importance of such activities; however, in many large, research-oriented institutions, the concept is maturing more slowly inside the committees that decide on tenure, promotion, and salary .

In response to my complaint about the great effort it takes to organize and present a really good *Science Bag* program, my department chair suggested that if it takes so much effort, why didn't I change the expectations and settle for something that can be prepared in less time? It was not an unreasonable suggestion, but I knew that, complaints aside, I had no interest in going in that direction. Part of my response to that suggestion was identified by Georgia O'Keeffe in her answer to a slightly different question. When asked why she painted flowers so very big in a number of her paintings, she said that if she painted them smaller, she supposed that most people wouldn't notice them.

Sometimes we have struggled with getting enough publicity to fill the house, and other times we have had to turn away significant numbers of people on a Friday night. My records show that over the first twenty-five years we have had an average attendance of 202 people per night. That means that for every blizzardy January evening when only sixty people showed up, there were several other occasions when the audience filled the room. In April 1998 I gave the last program of the twenty-fifth year of *The Science Bag*. It was titled, "Sunlight and Ice Crystals in the Skies of Antarctica," not unrelated to the first program of the first year of the series. I took a few minutes at the end of my presentation to give some review of that first twenty-five years, during which we had 120,000 attenders. In closing I said that *The Science Bag* seemed to be off to a good start and it was time for me to turn it over to someone else.

We have produced videotape versions of selected *Science Bag* programs* to market to middle and high schools, colleges, and universities, and to museums and science centers around the country. I estimate that a third of a million students see one of those programs each year—perhaps not a negligible contribution to science education.

How do we measure the value of a *Science Bag* activity? I think that we have no good measure. There is sufficient anecdotal evidence to suggest that it has been important to quite a number of people. A parent mentions her daughter's fascination with a program given some years ago on Fibanocci numbers, and suggests a connection with the fact that the daughter is now an undergraduate majoring in mathematics. A young assistant professor at a Nebraska university identifies a colleague of mine at a meeting. She tells him that she grew up in Milwaukee, attending *Science Bag* programs, and that they were what led her into physics. Another parent reports the whispered comment of her eight-year-old boy after the final applause has faded: "Someday I'm going to give a talk like that." And a friend tells of an overheard conversation between two twelve-year-old boys which ended with one exclaiming, "How can something this good be free?"

Without such comments I might not have had the energy to keep it going. Although children are the subjects of many of these reported anecdotes, children do not constitute the main part of the audience. Our surveys show

---

* *Information about these videotapes can be obtained from the address on the last page of this book.*

that seventy percent of the audience is older than high-school age.

Closer to home I hear another story. My daughter, Robin, visiting us recently, attended the opening night of a *Science Bag* performance and was a part of the discussion afterwards—of the program, its problems, how it could be improved, and whether we should invest the resources to make a videotape version of it. She was very tuned in to the things that had worked well in the presentation and had good insight into changes in the presentation that would improve it. She is now, among her other identities, a wife, a mother, and a biologist who is involved in developing science projects for teachers. After we had worked over the evening's performance, Robin recalled her own involvement with *The Science Bag*.

She was twelve when we first started the programs, and for two of my presentations she served as my assistant, operating the slide projector and helping with demonstrations. But she saw her involvement as being considerably greater than that. She would regularly go to the performances and be a part of the discussions about the first night—what changes to suggest to the speaker to improve his or her presentation— and perhaps would return to a program later in the month to see how it developed. How has this experience influenced her involvement in science education? Maybe significantly. Who can really say?

I was invited to talk at a seminar arranged at the University of Nebraska by the professor of physics who had been inspired by *The Science Bag* when she was a girl in Milwaukee. I told the assembled group that I hoped Diandra would not be insulted by something I wanted to say, but I thought that the most important influences of this program were possibly not on the Diandras whose career choices were influenced by *The Science Bag*. It might well be that the most important results were the changes in the attitude of nonscientists in our society toward science.

> **"We rarely missed a program until our kids grew up and left home,"** says the woman, who knows me from seeing most of the twenty-two different programs I have presented over the years. **"Then, after a year of missing the programs, my husband and I realized that we enjoyed those programs so much that we didn't need to have the kids as an excuse to attend, so we started to come again by ourselves."** And that is not the first time I have heard that identical story.

Chapter Seven

MICHAEL FARADAY AND THE ROYAL INSTITUTION

We have been in the library only a few minutes when the Marshall's staff strikes the floor three times, and he announces in stentorian tones, "It is now eight fifty-eight." Following tradition, our small party then moves the few steps down the hall to the lecture room. The dignitaries take their seats. The President of the Royal Institution (His Royal Highness, the Duke of Kent) is not in attendance tonight, so Barbara is escorted on the arm of a senior member of the Council into the filled room, to one of two gilded chairs on a slightly raised platform just in front of the lecture bench. The doors flanking the lecture bench close once more. Peter Day, director of the Royal Institution, stands outside one of them and I, outside the other. While we wait the interminable seconds, I keep telling myself not to enter the room and say, "Good evening, ladies and gentlemen," and yet am not sure that I will be able to avoid it. The clock strikes and the doors fly open. I have no idea of what happens to Peter Day, but I step to the bench, and "without prefatory remarks of any kind" start my Friday Evening Discourse on "Sunlight, Ice Crystals, and Sky Archaeology."

These Friday Evening Discourses at the Royal Institution of Great Britain (RI), located at 21 Albemarle Street in London, have been going on since Michael Faraday started them in 1826. Faraday's life is an amazing story of a poor apprentice to a bookbinder who, through self-education, became one of the prominent figures in the development of science. If Nobel Prizes were offered in his day, he certainly would have merited at least two. One prize would be in physics for his development of the connection between electricity and magnetism, and one would be in chemistry for his development of the fundamental ideas that are the basis for what is today called electrochemistry. Faraday's career is also inextricably tied up with the development of the Royal Institution.

His ghost is alive and well at the Royal Institution, and many of the traditions that determine how things are done at the RI can be traced to Faraday's influence. He was convinced that when we talk of science to public audiences, it is important to use demonstrations as part of the presentation ". . . for though to all true philosophers science and nature will have charms innumerable in every dress," he said, "yet I am sorry to say the generality of mankind cannot accompany us one short hour unless the path is strewed with flowers."

In preparation for my presentation I had shipped a large crate of "flowers" ahead and had spent the afternoon setting up and practicing the demonstrations so that, in this new setting, they would work smoothly, without complication.

Faraday understood well the difficulty of bringing the discourse and the demonstrations together into a smooth presentation, and he thought it to be totally unreasonable to expect a speaker to meet and carry on casual conversation with guests just before such an evening performance. Instead, he would escort the speaker to a small room for the half hour preceding the nine o'clock beginning of the Discourse, where he or she could concentrate on the upcoming delivery.

According to local legend Charles Wheatstone was to deliver a Discourse in 1846. Apparently Wheatstone was more at ease in his laboratory than in talking with people and, as he waited in the small room, thinking about the four hundred people sitting in the lecture room dressed for the event, awaiting his appearance, he became more and more uneasy until, a few minutes before 9:00 P.M., he walked out of the front door of the Royal Institution—and did not come back. The story is that Faraday, faced with an assembled audience and no speaker, talked a bit about Wheatstone's work and then described some of his own current experiments.

After that experience, he continued the tradition of giving the speaker half an hour of solitude before the talk—with one small change. After the speaker was escorted to the small room, the door was closed and the key was turned, locking him in. This, then, became a part of the tradition. I was told the story of Wheatstone before I was taken to Faraday's office, still furnished with Faraday's desk, chair, and couch, and with his books and some of his apparatus, and I noted the key hanging in the door. The key was not turned, I suppose in compliance with modern fire regulations, but I wondered if it were only a coincidence that the assistant to the lecturer had a desk commanding a view of the hall leading away from Faraday's office.

A British friend pointed out to me that the dinner jacket was the usual informal dress for the people who came out to hear Faraday's lectures in the middle nineteenth century, but no one has bothered to tell the Royal Institution that it is no longer the usual dress. My instructions for the event informed me that the lecturer would wear formal attire. For the audience the instructions were slightly more permissive. Their instructions: "While evening dress (dinner jacket) is not obligatory, the Council would like guests to know that it is customary." Most of the men in the audience appeared in the "customary" dress, while the women appeared to have a choice less specified. I solved my problem of dress with a visit to the venerable Moss Bros. establishment on Regent Street.

The real reason for many of the customs at the RI is TRADITION, but of course, there is also a rationalization that goes with each. Why is the talk to begin without any introduction of the speaker or with the speaker giving no "prefatory remarks of any kind," as was stated in my instructions? The rationalization is that the printed program gives sufficient information about the speaker and there is, hence, no need for an introduction. Other intellectual or artistic performances, such as plays or concerts, are not preceded by small talk from the director or conductor, so there is no place for that here.

A comment on this tradition is made in an oil painting by the physicist C. E. S. Phillips, who served as the Honorary Secretary of the RI from

1929 to 1945. The painting, hanging in Faraday's Office, shows a lecturer standing behind the bench, beaming pleasantly at the audience in the RI lecture room. But the audience is in a state of great agitation, with some men holding up their hands as if to stop the proceedings. Other horrified men and women gasp at what is going on, and two have fainted from the shock. Someone runs from behind to physically restrain the smiling speaker who, eyes half closed, is unaware of the crisis he has provoked. All is explained by the title of the painting, which is printed on a strip of cardboard affixed to the gilded frame. The first part of the title has been torn off, presumably to protect the guilty. It reads: *[   ] WHO ACCIDENTALLY SAID "LADIES AND GENTLEMEN" AT THE RI.*

My presentation, on this March evening in 1993, is about optical effects in the sky that result from the interaction of sunlight with falling ice crystals. I have many beautiful slides of these effects, and our computer simulations provide visual confirmation of the explanations. Along with Faraday I have long been convinced of the value of lecture demonstrations and have developed some very pretty demonstrations to help explain these optical effects. I have given enough talks about this subject to be quite familiar with the material. One tradition of the Royal Institution Friday Evening Discourses, however, makes giving this talk a difficult task.

The presentation started exactly on the stroke of 9 P.M., and I was clearly led to understand that *it should not go beyond the stroke of 10.* People laughed about that tradition when they told of a recent Discourse on music, when the speaker started to play a nine-minute piano composition at five minutes before 10, and so she obviously ran past the hour. But *several* people did tell me of the incident. I understood that while one should not exceed one hour (read: one hr. 00 min. 00 sec.), a shorter performance is acceptable. However, the absolute best performance is one in which the last sentence is finished just as the clock in the lecture room strikes 10. The British comment on such a performance would be, "Good show!"

One gets another clue to the seriousness of this tradition when he is shown that, in addition to the chiming clock on the wall, there is on the podium, clearly visible only to the speaker, a digital clock and an analog clock. One of the duties of the assistant is, on the afternoon of the lecture, to synchronize both of these clocks with the wall clock, the source of Royal Institution Standard Time.

My difficulty with timing arose from the inclusion in my talk of "Sky Archaeology," a topic centered on a complex display of ice-crystal halos, arcs, circles, streaks, and spots that filled the sky over the city of St. Petersburg, Russia, on June 18, 1790. Tobias Lowitz recorded the event in a drawing and later published the drawing and a description of the display, without any speculation as to its origins. Since then people who have looked into the role of airborne ice crystals in optical manifestations of the sky have understood some of the elements of that display. In fact, it has drawn the attention of those of us who try to understand such effects—as a test of our understanding. After working, slowly, through the simulations of sun pillars, sun dogs, upper and lower tangent arcs, circumzenithal arcs, Parry arcs, and many others, we were finally drawn, as moths to the candle, to the St. Petersburg display as the final exam in the course of our investigation. While some of the elements in Lowitz's drawing were well known and understood, others had eluded all attempts at explanation.

Several ice-crystal effects change their shape dramatically as the elevation of the sun above the horizon changes. In Lowitz's drawing both the twenty-two- and forty-six-degree halos are unmistakable, and from them we can see that the sun is about fifty degrees above the horizon. My students and I decided to do a master simulation, plotting everything we suspected might have contributed to the St. Petersburg display for the fifty-degree sun elevation. At this time we could only do these simulations on the University's main computer and have them plotted with wet ink on thirty-inch paper. The plotting time was a few hours, and we waited impatiently for the computing center to work through their queue of jobs until they could get to ours.

Two days after we requested the plot, we finally got the call saying that it was done. A couple of students were in my office when we unrolled the large sheet of paper, and as we looked at all the sky effects combined, some new insights leapt from the sheet. We were in the midst of the excitement over this new understanding when my recently arrived Polish colleague, Ryszard, came to the door and was puzzled by the animated display of exuberance he faced. He was involved with studying the structures of molecules stuck on surfaces and did not know about St. Petersburg.

"What are you doing?" he asked.

"Look . . . Lowitz . . . St. Petersburg . . . 1790 . . . nobody understands . . . right there, the Lowitz Arcs . . . ," we sputtered.

As he began to piece together what was going on, he exclaimed, "Why, you are doing sky archeology!"

It seemed an apt comment, and we have continued to use that term to refer to our attempts at understanding old records of sky effects.

We did not completely unravel the puzzle on that first attempt, but several clues led us finally to understand the difficulty of explaining this record from 1790. We, and others, had assumed that Lowitz was showing us a snapshot of what he saw that day. But it became clear to us that he was doing something else. He was adding to his master drawing everything he saw from when he started observing at seven-thirty in the morning until the display disappeared shortly after noon. No doubt the display waxed and waned, disappearing and reappearing as the morning progressed, and Lowitz recorded, on the same drawing, the same effect with drastically different shapes resulting from different elevations of the sun at different times in the morning. He recorded, on the same drawing, effects that never would appear together at the same time.

During the course of that detective work we came to understand things that Lowitz had seen and recorded but had not himself understood. In addition, we gained several little insights about particular things that the man must have done on that June day, two centuries earlier, as he stood and marveled at the beauty he saw in the sky of St. Petersburg. It was a most satisfying result.

The problem at the Royal Institution was that if I wanted to include the adventures of Tobias Lowitz in St. Petersburg (and I intended to), I had to precede that episode with a development of the sources of the various arcs and halos that made up the display. Without that development the audience would not appreciate the St. Petersburg mystery—or its denouement. When I had tried to do that with other groups it had taken more than an hour. If the audience were sufficiently engrossed in the plot, the extra five or seven minutes was not fatal. However, I had not given one of Michael Faraday's Friday Evening Discourses at the Royal Institution of Great Britain on Albemarle Street in London before.

Actually, I had been preparing for this talk for the last twenty years. *The Science Bag* was the preparation. In the context of my efforts to bring science to the public in Milwaukee, the invitation to give a Friday Evening Discourse at the Royal Institution seemed like a call to visit the "home office." The Discourses and the Christmas Lectures were both started by Michael Faraday in 1826. The Christmas Lectures are a set of five lectures on related topics given by a distinguished scientist for students during the Christmas school recess.

In the early days of television the BBC started to produce these programs, and they are now seen on television each year by most of the school children in England. Both the Discourses and the Christmas Lectures have continued from Faraday's introduction to this day and are probably the most prestigious efforts of this kind of public science education in the world. In describing my efforts in this field to Peter Day, the Director of the Royal Institution who invited me to participate, I pointed out that in 127 more years, *The Science Bag* would have been in operation half as long as the Friday Evening Discourses. That does provide a certain perspective.

I was aware of these programs at the Royal Institution, and they probably did influence my thinking about public education in science. To accompany my Friday Evening presentation, the RI mounted a large exhibit in the library. It included much additional material on optical sky effects, a display of all of my scientific publications and other career involvements, and a prominent description of *The Science Bag* series, including programs, photos, and a continuously running video with excerpts from various *Science Bag* presentations. The person arranging the exhibit asked if it were all right if, on an information poster about *The Science Bag*, she were to say that the Royal Institution's programs were the inspiration for *The Science Bag*. Of course.

So some things are different, but the process is familiar. I have spent a lot of effort learning how to introduce people

to a new topic, catch their interest, teach them some basic concepts, offer the reward of using these concepts to understand a new effect, and help them appreciate the beauty. Tonight the audience is responsive and ready to register their appreciation. They really like the spinning-prism, sun-dog demonstration. They are eager to accept my challenge to predict the orientation of a falling ice crystal. They are a bit shocked, at least surprised, when I climb up onto the lecture bench to drop some spinning cards—laughter and applause—yes, that was the right decision; they didn't expect that of an old guy in formal clothes, and it helped renew their attention.

The clock is the biggest worry. I have cut out all the topics, no matter how interesting, not essential to my main story. I resist the temptation to tell how physicists don't do as well on the falling-crystal predictions as do pedestrians. I don't elaborate on the search for infralateral arcs . . . don't point out the faint supralateral arcs in that photo of Ohtake's . . . it would just take a few seconds. No, don't do it . . . skip the New Mexico story . . . tighten up Lowitz's description of how the display changed over the day . . . on the overhead projector, build up the simulation of St. Petersburg, one effect at a time, but keep it moving. . . . What did Lowitz do on that day?. . . what else?. . . how must he have felt? . . . don't you think that's interesting? . . . Applause. The Duke of Kent, in this case his substitute, comes forward, as is the tradition, to shake my hand, formally ending the presentation. I check the clock. Oh no! I overcompensated—I finished with eight minutes to spare!

Chapter Eight

BEEKEEPING

First I've got to organize all this stuff and find out what's here, throw out some of it, and inventory the rest. Then organize it, figure out what it's worth, and announce a sale. I'll sort out the small amount of equipment I'll keep to use with my few colonies of bees, but the rest of it has to be dealt with. What's in those comb supers under the stack of queen excluders? Old combs, predictably riddled with the webby remains of wax moths—what a mess! They should have been melted or thrown out long ago. The frames are so scarred with the depressions left by the wax-moth pupae that I should probably burn the whole lot. Should I do that now or pile them somewhere and do it later? Somehow this seems to be almost more than I can cope with. What's going on?

For several years my father had not been able to do the work to care for the four colonies of bees he kept in his back yard. He had sold the nearly two hundred colonies located in ten different bee yards that he had at the height of his beekeeping, but he had kept these four colonies. I was living in Wisconsin, four hundred miles away from his home in northwestern Ohio, so I couldn't provide the care they needed. A local beekeeper tended them as a favor and brought him some honey each year. Why hadn't he gotten rid of these last four colonies? Actually, I understood it at the time, and understand it even better now.

My father had started keeping bees as a hobby in his early twenties and had kept, observed, experimented with, read about, and studied bees for over fifty years. They had been a continuing object of his attention, and he had made his interest into a part-time job. It fit well with his job as a schoolteacher, since the bees required the most attention in the summer, when he had the time to devote to them. If he were to get rid of those last four colonies, it would mean accepting, or at least acknowledging, his physical limitations in a way that he did not want to do.

And he did get some benefit from them. On a spring day he could get outside and watch the bees flying from the entrances of the hives. He could see the worker bees dragging out of the hive bees that had died over the winter and, from the number of bees flying, he could contemplate the strength of the remaining colony.

Some of the incoming bees would have large clumps of pollen easily visible on their back legs, and from the golden or yellow or white or pink color of the pollen he might identify the plants from which it came. He could see a bee, flying to the entrance of the hive without pollen but landing heavily on the bottom board, and know that it was full of nectar. At this time of the year they wouldn't be storing any amount of excess honey, but the pollen and honey from the early blossoms were essential for raising new bees to rapidly build up the strength of the colony from the few thousand that lived over the winter to the sixty thousand or so that would gather and store a good crop of honey in June and July. The early intake of pollen and nectar, very dependent on weather conditions, was critical to the population buildup and, hence, to the success of the colony.

And, given a piece of bad luck, he might detect a faint odor that indicated a disease of the bees in the hive, so serious that sometimes the beekeeper would kill the bees and burn the combs to prevent the spread of the disease to other colonies. Even without taking the cover off the hive, he was able to participate in the life of the bee colony just by his observations of the activity at the hive entrance.

My mother had been unsuccessful in her efforts to get my father to dispose of the equipment that filled the honey house, equipment that he would never again use. When he died, a few months ago, I told her that I would take care

of it all; she didn't need to worry about it. I would sort through it, organize it, and have a sale. And here I am struggling with the process, having a great deal of difficulty with the whole business. I keep thinking about my father.

His name was Dallas, and it surprised me when people thought it a strange name. It was even more surprising if someone associated the name with the soap-opera stereotype of a Texas millionaire. He was fairly tall and lean, a quiet, even-tempered man. I don't remember when I began accompanying him on his trips to care for the bees; it seems that I always did. In the busiest part of the summer we would spend two or three days each week driving to the bee yards, examining each colony, responding to problems we found, and hauling supers (boxes of empty combs) out to the bee yard to provide space for the bees to store this year's honey crop.

When I was a teenager I could do my share of the work, examining the hives in one row as he worked the next, and we talked together about any unusual condition that required our attention. At age fourteen I got a driver's license that allowed me to take the car and trailer to bring the loads of equipment we needed at each bee yard. Thinking about it now, I am a bit surprised at his having a fourteen-year-old do that job, but it seemed perfectly reasonable to me at the time.

The original bee yard was at one end of the woods. After we finished caring for the bees, we would take a walk through the woods. Through the distorting lens of my memory I see those walks as providing the beginnings of a way of looking at nature that has affected my perception of the world ever since.

We, of course, would look for the spring wild flowers and see if they occurred in the same place and time as last year. It was a great treat to find "sponge mushrooms" (morels) after a warm spring rain. Morels are considered by some mushroom fanciers to be the most desirable of species, and we would take our treasure home, even if we found only two or three. My mother, without fail, would admire our find and fry them in butter, even if it yielded only a taste for each of the five of us, including my two older sisters. It was a sort of spring ritual that we enjoyed. Her attitude was the same toward the tiny, sweet, wild strawberries which, considering the work involved in their preparation, must have been valued more for the ritual than for their nutrition.

When a rabbit jumped out of a pile of brush and zigzagged off through the woods, we watched him run until he dove into another brush pile. "Let's see where he goes next," said my father. After a time we spooked him out of his second refuge, and in the course of our circuit of the woods we were able to follow him from one hiding place to the next, until he returned to the brush pile where we originally found him. Does that suggest that he doesn't just run and look for a place to hide, but has some places of refuge all figured out?

There were a few small juniper bushes in the woods near our bee yard. My father observed that they had been about the same size for the past twenty years and speculated on whether it had to do with the sheep that were occasionally let in to graze. The sheep didn't seem to like the juniper, but they were not above trying a taste just to be sure they didn't like it.

One of my first entrepreneurial ventures came from those woods. The farmer had cleared a corner of the woods by uprooting bushes and small trees with his tractor. In the tangle of branches and roots, piled up for burning, were several sassafras trees. The bark of the root of that tree has, to my perception, one of the best fragrances to be found in this world. Fresh or dried, the root bark can be boiled in water to produce a wonderful tea. I sawed the roots off the trees and took them home. After scrubbing the roots and peeling the bark, I tied it in fragrant bundles, which I took to small local grocery stores. A usual reaction was for the grocer to exclaim, "I haven't smelled that since I was a boy!" and take a dozen bundles.

After a winter with heavy snow my father might point out a bush with some of the bark removed. But the bark was only gone from the branches in the top part of the bush; in fact, the region of bark damage is bounded by a smooth plane sloping through the bush. He would point out that the rabbits would only chew on the branches that extended up above the snow surface and, with that boundary, we could see the shape of the snow drift through the bush, in the hungry part of the winter, as clearly as if we had been there. Sometimes the observations were connected with things that happened in the past and sometimes in the present.

When bees are busy gathering nectar, they are gentle to handle. Too early in the morning or in the evening or on rainy days, when they cannot be about their business of making honey, they are very testy and hard to handle. By being "hard to handle" I refer to a whole set of behaviors, one characteristic being that they want to sting any intruder. I remember a few days when we worked the bees with no difficulty until, around noon, something changed. Although the sun was still out, the bees became irritable and we were getting stung.

What was going on? My father frequently would examine flowering plants in the vicinity of a bee yard to see what they were working on, to see the source of their nectar or pollen. He had heard or read that there are plants that will only yield nectar during some part of the day. He associated this strange bee behavior with his observation that on those days the bees were very busy in the morning, working the blossoms of a lush plant called knotweed or heartsease. Around noon they quit working that plant, and his surmise was that the knotweed quit yielding nectar in midday and, as a result, the disgruntled bees returned to the hive in a bad mood.

I don't know whether that was the right explanation for what happened, but it was an attempt to see beyond the immediate observation, which was typical of his approach. It was his attempt to see with the mind as well as with the eye. I see it as the beginning of my habit of viewing the world with questioning eyes, a habit that I consciously try to cultivate. I suspect that this habit is responsible for a significant part of whatever success I have had in my scientific endeavors.

I was specifically reminded of that approach I take to seeing the world when I was at the Fritz Haber Institute in Berlin. I worked mainly on surface science but did a bit of investigation with the electron-microscope group, looking at butterfly wings and abalone shells. In some butterfly wings the colors do not come from the usual pigments that absorb part of the light spectrum and scatter other parts back to your eye. Rather, the colors result from some submicroscopic structures that produce the colors by the interference of light waves. A familiar example of this effect is the colors that result from a thin, transparent layer of oil on the surface of water, or the colors seen in the light reflected from a soap bubble.

While I was in Berlin, I gave a general colloquium on this topic, titled,

"Beetles, Bubbles, and Butterflies: Iridescence in Nature." I showed many examples of interference colors in bird feathers, beetle shells, butterfly wings, paua shells, spider webs, and other biological structures where it was clear that the colors were interference colors. However, in most cases, we did not know what kind of structure produces the effects. After that talk Karsten Horn, a colleague in the surface work, said to me, "I have seen many of those things that you showed, but it never occurred to me that there were questions to be asked. You help to open our eyes." Seeing the question is the beginning of understanding. Frequently there are more people who can answer a well-posed question than there are people who can see and pose the question. I associate my education in "seeing" with those walks in the woods with my father.

Of course, all the lessons about seeing that I learned from my father did not take place in the woods where the bees were located, but I think of the experiences there as symbolic of that part of our relationship. I do know that we always had time, after the work was done, for the walk through the woods. Sometimes, when there was much to do and time was tight, it was only a short walk, but the walk was an unspoken part of the deal. It was similar to the deal that whenever we went past the good ice cream place in Fremont, we would stop for ice cream cones. Since we frequently went through Fremont both going and coming, it meant two stops for cones—all part of the deal.

As I got older and went through that standard part of growing up when we try to differentiate ourselves from our parents, I saw some of my father's shortcomings with all the clarity of a sixteen-year-old's acute vision. He was not a putterer; he did not enjoy fixing up this and painting that and doing small maintenance jobs. When he removed a frame containing a honeycomb from the hive and the top bar pulled loose, he might comment that he should put a nail in it one of these days. To myself I might say, "Yes, but you never will. If I were in charge of this bee yard, I would do things differently." There was a point at which I realized that in a couple of years I was probably not going to be a part of this activity. I would be leaving home and having summer jobs, and it was really going to be my father's business. If we were going to develop a partnership, we would have to work some things out, but given the situation, I should really consider it his business.

It is interesting to see in myself, as an adult, a number of those same characteristics that I criticized in my father.

> I find myself sitting among this old equipment and thinking about my father, and all of a sudden I realize why I am having so much difficulty dealing with it. It is so strongly associated with both the good times and the difficult times I had with him, that trying to sort out this stuff now is like reworking that important part of our relationship. So that's what's going on! Well, now I guess that I can get on with the job of dealing with all of this stuff.

Is beekeeping one of the traditions in my life? Two generations might be barely enough to start a tradition, but I can see beyond that. My daughter, Karen, and her partner, Penny, are enthusiastic beekeepers, as is my son-in-law, John, and daughter-in-law, Susan. Our get-together in the fall to extract the honey from all of our hives is one of the rituals of the season. And when I see their small children watch the bees with great interest, I do have the sense of a tradition.

Chapter Nine

MIRAGES

The Japanese television producer seems very serious about producing a two-hour program on mirages for Tokyo television. He has brought an interpreter with him to make our conversation possible and is willing to take camera crews to sites around the world to get good footage of mirage effects.

He knew of my interest in mirages through my book and other publications and asked to come and talk with me about mirages. I suggested he come to Toronto, where I was to give a lecture-demonstration presentation, "The Mirage, the Discovery of Greenland, and the Green Flash," at the annual meeting of the Optical Society of America. I had given the presentation that morning, and it came off fairly well, considering the usual range of difficulties one encounters in putting on a complicated show in a strange auditorium.

For instance, the people in charge of fire protection in the Convention Center were very concerned because I was going to use fire in one of my demonstrations. I planned to use one hundred, one-inch-high flames, fueled by propane from a small bottle, to heat a nine-foot-long model desert. They finally agreed to my doing it if they had a firefighter standing by with a fire extinguisher. We also found solutions to the camera tripod that wouldn't go low enough, the tabletop demonstrations that, on the elevated stage, couldn't be seen by people in the front rows, etc., etc. After some rather tense times all came together, and the audience seemed quite appreciative.

So now we are meeting for coffee and conversation about mirages. The producer is very interested in the fata morgana mirages that I had photographed over the Arctic Ocean from Point Barrow, Alaska. At what time of year could he take a camera crew there to capture that effect? Very hard to say. Such effects don't exactly appear on command, and I don't even have a good feeling about how often (or how seldom) those effects occur. I happened to capture them while I was there looking for ice-crystal effects, I say.

He also wants to know where I had photographed the hot-road-mirage effects that had been a part of my presentation. There are, no doubt, many places in the southwest, I tell him, where such displays are commonly seen, although I can't give him any specific locations. However, it is surprisingly difficult to find a really flat stretch of road even in a part of the country that seems rather flat. In the upper midwest the flattest stretch of road that I have found is in the Upper Peninsula of Michigan, where my hot-road-mirage photographs were taken. Where is that? I take a napkin and sketch a map of the five Great Lakes. For reference I mark Toronto on Lake Ontario, where we are having coffee, and Chicago on Lake Michigan, because most people have heard of Chicago. Warming to the idea, I add Milwaukee, where I live, and draw a small square, representing the location of a primitive cabin we have built in the bush, a mile from the northern shore of Lake Huron. To get to that cabin, I drive across Michigan's Upper Peninsula and, on sunny days, examine the hot-road mirages on some long stretches of flat road. On the map I locate the Upper Peninsula and represent the long, flat road with a straight line, unavoidably out of scale. He looks at the napkin with apparent interest.

Actually, my life has been intertwined with the Great Lakes. I grew up near Lake Erie, before the days when pollution there was an obvious problem. That lake was a part of the swimming, fishing, picnicking, and beach-walking activities of my childhood. As a student at the University of Rochester I was within easy reach of Lake Ontario and enjoyed its shores on weekend hikes. We now live a mile from Lake Michigan, have

Chapter Nine: **MIRAGES**

The two motorcycles and the car with their apparent reflections, illustrating
the hot-road or desert mirage.

The nine-foot-long, heated plate that produces a model-desert mirage.

(Photo by Alan Magayne Roshak)

Views across the model desert. Successive photos show the desert scene from the viewpoints closer and closer to the plane of the desert floor. As the viewpoint is lowered, the vanishing line in the desert scene rises, giving the appearance of the scene being submerged in the desert lake. An apparent reflection takes place about the vanishing line.

A. The scene without mirage effects.

B. The vanishing line is below the horizon, resulting in the appearance of a lake between the observer and the scene.

C. The vanishing line is slightly above the horizon, cutting off the wheels of the Volkswagen and giving the impression that the camel is standing in water.

D. The vanishing line is above the VW, and the camel appears to be belly deep in the water of the mirage lake.

A version of the fata morgana mirage in which there appears to be a wall of ice standing out beyond the ice-research shack. The photo was taken looking out over the Arctic Ocean from Point Barrow, Alaska.

Another of the many forms of the fata morgana seen from Point Barrow.

A laser beam taking a curved path through a tank containing a layer
of fresh water over salt water.
(Photo by Alan Magayne-Roshak)

Three views of the drawing of a ship (Figure A), as seen through the tank in the top photo,
showing classical, superior-mirage effects.

B. A view showing the effect known to the seafaring as "towering."
C. A view from a different height showing "stooping."
D. A three-part mirage, often reported in old records. Here it is faithfully
reproduced by a view through the mirage tank.

Chapter Twelve: JUST PLAYING

Cabin on the edge of a rock outcropping.

Cabin in winter. (Can you figure out the connection between the pattern of snow on the roof and the icicle curtain over the front porch?)

Spider webs, as seen looking out from the front porch. These webs later became the subject of an article titled, "Colors in Spider Webs" in the July-August 1989 issue of *American Scientist*.

A long soap bubble.

(Photo by Raymond F. Newell, Jr.)

A bubble, approximately one meter in diameter, floating over the rock. Note the images of trees and sky in the bubble and the interference colors in the thin soap films.
(Photo by Raymond F. Newell, Jr.)

Top spinners from Kota Baru, Malaysia.
The master spinner, winding the rope tightly around his seven-pound top.
(Malaysian photos by K. Bruce Jacobson)

The author trying to scoop up the spinning top.

A member of the top-spinning team, meditating on the top before he sets it into a bamboo section partially buried in the ground. Typically such a top will remain spinning for an hour or more.

taken several trips along Superior's beautiful shores, and have built a small cabin just back from the shore of the North Channel of Lake Huron. I took some secret pride in being able to rapidly sketch the map for my Japanese producer as he was asking details of the location of that road in Michigan.

My interest in water is not confined to the Great (or lesser) Lakes. I can trace a fascination with water back to my earliest memories. I am told that one of my first words was a child's attempt to say "water," and I showed excitement when, riding in the car, we crossed a bridge over a river, or even a country creek. Only a few years ago I realized that I still have remnants of that early excitement. As I approach a country creek while driving or riding in a car, I invariably make a decision of whether I will look down the creek, or up the creek, or will try for a quick look in both directions. I have been doing that unconsciously for years, without realizing it, and it has something to do with the excitement and mystery that a stream still holds for me. (I would vote to revoke the license of any civil engineer who designs a bridge with solid railings that hide the river from the view of people in passing cars.)

But I was talking about mirages. In general, we can divide mirages into two classes. One example of the most familiar class is the desert mirage, or the hot-road mirage, which occurs when the sun heats the desert or road to a higher temperature than the air. The air right at the surface is quite hot, but if you measure its temperature at different heights above the surface, you find that it drops significantly in the first few inches or feet. A result of this temperature gradient (the change of temperature with height) is that a light ray passing through the air follows a curved path.

Intuitively you assume that light travels in a straight line, and if asked to point to the location of an object, you will point in the direction from which the light ray approaches your eye. When a light ray from a distant object gets to your eye by a curved path that sags in the middle (like a rope held at both ends), the ray enters your eye coming slightly up from below. To point to the object you would point along that line and actually be pointing below its real position. This is the situation in the atmosphere when the air temperature is decreasing with height; the apparent position of a distant object is below its real position. From that apparent lowering we give the name to this class of mirages: inferior mirages. The term, inferior, is no aesthetic or moral judgment; it only refers to the lowered apparent position of a distant object.

Other, more interesting features are a part of a desert mirage. When you are standing on the solar-heated sand of the desert floor, you can see a frond on a distant palm tree via a light ray that follows a slightly curved path to your eye. If your eye is five feet above the sand surface, the ray gets to your eye on a path that never takes it much closer to the surface than five feet. The air temperature is changing rapidly at the surface but changing only slowly five feet above the surface. The slight curvature lowers the apparent position of the palm frond by such a small amount that it will not be noticed.

However, another light ray from the frond gets to your eye following a very different path. A ray that nearly grazes the desert floor gets bent strongly (because the temperature change is rapid near the surface) and comes up to your eye from a direction below the horizon. The result of these two ray paths, from palm frond to your eye, is that you can see the palm frond about where you expect it to be and also below the horizon. If we trace rays from different parts of the palm tree, we realize that the part seen below the horizon is in the form of an inverted image of the tree. Amazing! Because of the temperature gradient in the air, you see a (more-or-less) normal image of the tree and, below it, an inverted image.

Your mind always tries to make sense out of the visual images presented to it by the eye, and this one is easy to interpret. The only other place in nature where you see a tree sitting above its inverted image is when you view it over a water surface and see its reflection. So what you perceive is water in the distant desert. What you really see is an apparent reflection—an inverted image of objects and sky—that your mind interprets as seeing water. I call it an apparent *reflection* because the light rays are not really reflected, changing their direction discontinuously at a specific point in their paths, but are *refracted*, following a smooth curve through the air as a result of the temperature gradient.

There are other interesting characteristics of an inferior mirage. As you move farther away from the palm tree in the desert, the lower part of the tree begins to disappear. There is a "vanishing line" that rises on the tree as you move away. The tree above the vanishing line is apparently reflected at that line, and you can see no part of the tree that lies below the line. In a desert this leads to the spooky situation where two people can be relatively close to each other, but under strong mirage conditions, each may be below the other's vanishing line and, hence, invisible.

Alistair Fraser, a meteorologist at Penn State University, makes the convincing case for the crossing of the Red Sea by the Israelites, described in the book of Exodus, being a mirage effect. In the midst of a desert, under conditions that produce a strong mirage, a person would seem to be standing on dry ground, surrounded by water on all sides. ". . . the children of Israel went into the midst of the sea upon the dry ground. . . and saw that the waters. . . were a wall unto them on their right hand and on their left . . ." sounds like a description of a desert mirage.

Fraser also points out that this thirty-two-hundred-year-old account is remarkable in its accurate description of the diurnal variation of the mirage. At night, as the desert cooled, the mirage would weaken, the vanishing line would lower and the water would appear to be farther away. We can read, "Moses stretched out his hand over the sea; and the Lord caused the sea to go back by a strong east wind," and later, "Moses stretched forth his hand over the sea and the sea returned to his strength when the morning appeared." With the mirage strengthening in the morning, "the waters returned and covered . . . all the host of Pharaoh." Of course, the Egyptians would have seen the Israelites "drowned" in the mirage and perhaps given up the pursuit. It would be interesting to find the Egyptian records of that incident.

These mirage effects were shown rather well, I thought, with my model desert at the Optical Society meeting in Toronto. I started by using a video camera to view the picture of an oasis placed at the far end of the heated model desert. The video image, projected on the large screen of the Convention Center stage, let each person in the audience "see" the oasis through the hot desert air. With the video camera raised slightly above the plane of the hot desert, everyone could see the scene of traditional palm trees and camel, supplemented with a red Volkswagen beetle and an oil derrick. The screen was filled with the desert image, writhing under the heat-wave distortion that is a familiar part of a real desert scene. Already it looked convincing.

Then, as the camera was lowered, a vanishing line appeared on the sand, showing a pool of water below the horizon—the appearance of the lake that gives false hope to thirsty desert travelers. With continued lowering of the camera, the vanishing line rises until the water stretches to the horizon. When the vanishing line rises to the camel's belly, it looks as if it is standing belly-deep in water. Next the VW disappears below the line and, as the line rises further, only the camel's head appears above the water, seen as if it were reflected in the surface. A few moments later, even the head disappears—the camel apparently drowned beneath the rising water. The treetops and a part of the derrick remain, suspended in the sky, doubled by the mirror image in that wavering desert scene, until the tide finally submerges them, leaving only the empty desert sky. (As you might guess, I really like that demonstration.)

It might seem surprising that this effect is intimately connected with one that I experienced on a cold winter day in January. I went out on the ice of Lake Michigan and turned back to look at the shore. Here, just north of Milwaukee, there are bluffs rising from the narrow beach. I saw the pattern formed by bare trees and bushes, areas of bare dirt and rocks, and patches of snow. But something looked strange in this pattern. Parts of the pattern above a horizontal line along the bluff were seen as if in reflection below the line. It looked as if there were a vanishing line and all of the features of a desert mirage.

As I recall, the temperature was several degrees below zero (Fahrenheit), and I had difficulty manipulating the camera equipment with my numb fingers. It didn't feel like my idea of the conditions for seeing a desert mirage. But consider the relative temperatures of the air and the surface. A few inches below the top surface of the ice was lake water at a temperature of thirty-two degrees. The ice was in intimate thermal contact with the water and was probably close to the water temperature, which was some forty degrees warmer than the air. It is the temperature *difference* that determines the paths of light rays, and I was seeing the same kind of inferior mirage that I would see in the desert. So hot air over a hotter desert, cool air over a warm lake, or frigid air over a frozen lake can all produce inferior mirages.

A second class of mirages results when the air temperature increases as you go up in the atmosphere. This can happen when the surface is colder than the air, or when, higher in the atmosphere, there is a temperature inversion. Light rays then follow an arching path through the atmosphere, with the rays coming down to your eye from above. One effect is an apparent raising of the position of an object above its true position, which gives rise to the name of this class of mirages: superior mirages. Again, this is no value judgment on mirages, merely a description of the apparent position of things you are viewing relative to their real position.

Travelers in the Arctic have reported this effect when they describe that the ice surface about them appears to rise in the distance, giving the impression that they are at the center of a vast, shallow bowl. The curved rays may enable a person to see distant ships or cities that would normally be hidden below the curve of the earth. Variations in the details of the temperature gradient may not lift an object, such as a distant ship, uniformly but may stretch or squash it in the vertical dimension. Old-time sailors call these effects "towering" and "stooping."

The most famous of these superior mirage effects has a name suggestive of magic and mystery: the fata morgana. The effect is named after Morgana, the half sister of King Arthur who, according to Celtic legend, has the powers of a fairy, which she exhibits through the mirage. Fata morgana, the Italian translation of Morgan the Fairy, is the name given to displays attributed in legend to her powers. Italian writers and poets described these effects as seen over the strait of Messina, between Italy and Sicily, and, although the effects occur worldwide, the name sticks. It was said that, out of thin air, she could create cities with castle walls and towers. We can understand these creations as superior mirages where short features in the distant landscape are vertically magnified into walls or towers.

It was my Alaskan photos of the fata morgana in which the Japanese producer expressed great interest. I was at the Naval Arctic Research Laboratory in Point Barrow over one vernal equinox. Point Barrow is the northernmost projection of Alaska, well within the Arctic Circle. On the equinox (equinox = equal nights) every place on earth has a twelve-hour day and twelve-hour night. At Point Barrow the sun followed a low path across the sky, never rising higher than about twenty degrees above the horizon. My excuse for being there was to pursue atmospheric ice-crystal effects, to look for them at the opposite end of the earth from my search the previous year in Antarctica. According to the best information I could get, this was the time of year when there were frequent ice-crystal displays. It is the time when leads (cracks) in the sea ice begin to appear and, presumably, the exposed sea surface in these leads provides the source of moisture necessary to produce a generous supply of small ice crystals in the cold air.

One day when I went to check the view over the Arctic Ocean, I was amazed to find the work of Morgana. For a while I could see a solid wall of ice rising abruptly from the rough sea ice, not far offshore. As the morning progressed, I watched pillars arising in the distance, sometimes in the form of delicate columns supporting more massive structures. These displays would change or even disappear as I walked up or down the slope next to the ocean, changing the height of my eye by only a few feet. I had telephoto lenses and a telescope to bring this display close to me, where I could examine its structure. But it took no stretch of the imagination to understand how someone without these aids could see, in such a display, the buildings and structures of a city on the distant horizon.

There is magic in the view of any distant horizon; the Fairy Morgan adds magic to magic. Do I believe in magic? It depends, of course, on how you define magic. My knowing how to trace rays through the atmosphere to give an explanation for the "structures" I witnessed in no way diminished my sense of awe in the display. I believe that the more I understand about mirages, the more I am moved by the wonder of their existence. I choose not, however, to make anything of the coincidence that the day Morgana chose to display her handiwork to me was the first of April.

I have found a very satisfying way to demonstrate the conditions that produce superior mirages. I first fill an aquarium half full of salt water, then carefully add a layer of fresh water. The lower density of the fresh water makes it form a stable layer on top of the salt water, with some mixing of the two at the boundary. After it sits for a day or so, a smooth transition develops between the layer of concentrated salt water on the bottom and the layer of fresh water on the top. The varying salt concentration in that transition region causes a light ray to take a curving path through the tank, curved in the same way as rays that produce a superior mirage in the atmosphere.

At my presentation in Toronto, with the Japanese producer in the audience, I had such a tank with salt and fresh water. I could shine a laser beam into one end of the tank and watch it pass through the tank and emerge from the other end. If I lowered the laser and pointed it slightly upward, the beam would move up to the salt-fresh transition layer and then follow a smooth curving path that turns the beam downward. The effect was so striking that I could shine the laser beam into the tank, pointing upwards, perhaps with a thirty-degree angle from the horizontal, and watch it follow a curved path emerging from the tank traveling downward at a thirty-degree angle. Looking through this exaggerated (very superior) atmosphere at various scenes, I could see them distorted into a variety of superior-mirage effects. If, instead of looking, I photographed the scene with the video camera and projected the image on the big screen, the audience could see all of the effects.

When I placed a picture of a sailing ship beyond the tank and viewed it through the tank with the camera in a specific position, I would see a squashed view of the ship. The old sailors would call the effect "stooping." By moving the camera slightly, I could find a position where the ship would be stretched vertically, magnified in only the vertical direction into a display known as "towering." Even more impressive was a camera position where an inverted image appeared above a normal-looking image of the ship—a ship floating upside down in the air above the "real" ship. To further confound the senses, there was yet a third image of the ship, an upright image in the sky, above the other two.

I arranged the camera position so that this three-part mirage display, produced by the water tank and projected on the big screen, gave a good match to some old drawings of a similar display made in 1797. The similarity was enhanced by the fact that I made the drawing of the ship to match the one in the display from 1797.

Actually, such three-part displays have been observed and described many times. The simplicity of the demonstration made it clear that it was not necessary to have two or three layers to get the three images; this could all be effected by the one region where the salt water below smoothly changed to the fresh water above. The corresponding change in a real atmosphere results from a change in the temperature of the air with height.

By viewing a drawing of a rough ice surface through the tank, I could also reproduce rather well some of the impressive Arctic photos of the fata morgana.

I had captured some of these dramatic mirage effects in slides, but there would be some additional interest in seeing the images shimmer and change with time, so recently I decided to have a try at capturing mirage effects on videotape. On a warm day in early spring the surface water in the Great Lakes can be considerably colder than the air, which gives the right conditions for superior mirages. A sunny day, with little wind, can produce hot-road mirages any time of year. I would take a leisurely trip to the cabin, looking for mirages over Lakes Michigan, Superior, and Huron en route. I would also try my luck on the flat, black-top road in the Upper Peninsula of Michigan.

A sequence that I hoped to capture on the hot road is one of a person walking off into the mirage, giving the appearance of walking into a sea of water until he finally disappears below its surface. As the person gets far enough away to disappear below the vanishing line of the mirage, the heat waves will distort the image rather badly, and I thought it might help if the person were dressed in some bold colors with, perhaps, a tall, flamboyant hat. I looked for some appropriate hat and costume without any success, until I decided to take the need for a costume seriously. Then I went with Barbara to a theatrical costume house, thinking that among their offerings I would find something that would help.

An Uncle Sam outfit seemed to have some real possibilities. It had a brightly colored stovepipe hat and the red-white-and-blue tail coat, vest, and pants. As I was imagining how it might work photographically, I began to think of the actual situation of walking along the hot road in this Uncle Sam outfit, some distance from the nearest town, in the Upper Peninsula, when the local sheriff comes cruising to a stop, rolls down his window, and asks, "How're ya doin' this afternoon?" I, of course, would have to explain that I had a video camera with a long telephoto lens back there by my car and was taking pictures of myself walking along this hot road . . . I was really interested in mirages. . . . and the outfit would make the photos more interesting. No, this was not the first time I tried to see mirages, I had done it a number of places around the country . . . even in Alaska and Antarctica . . . and I was feeling just fine, thank you. . . .

Just then Barbara came over to me, in the costume store, wearing a hat consisting of a pile of fruit—bananas, grapes, apples, peaches—and suggested that this Carmen Miranda getup was just the costume for me. I said to her, "I've just been thinking how I'm going to explain to the Upper Peninsula Sheriff why I'm walking down the road in an Uncle Sam outfit. At least he will have to have some respect for Uncle Sam. But if he finds me crossdressing as Carmen Miranda, I won't have a chance in the world of staying out of jail!"

I rented the Uncle Sam suit and headed on my mirage expedition. At Lake Superior I sat for a day in the fog and had generally overcast weather at the other lake sites. When the sun did shine, the wind was blowing enough to dissipate the hot-air layer and cool the blacktop road. I came back without any good mirage photos and never even took Uncle Sam out of the box. At least I didn't have to deal with the sheriff.

So the Japanese television producer has seen some of my bag of tricks. He is very interested in where and when he can film these mirages and, although I am willing to help, I find it difficult to help with his plan to set up a shooting schedule that will capture the mirages. He is polite and thanks me for my help, then asks if he may have the napkin, with the map sketch. Of course. After he leaves, I smile as I imagine a group of serious people around a table in Tokyo, with the napkin and an atlas of road maps of North America, trying to locate that straight, flat road in Michigan's Upper Peninsula.

Chapter Ten

SURFACE SCIENCE

When I answer the phone, I am surprised to find that it is someone with whom I have not talked in years. George Blyholder wants to know if I would be part of a symposium at the next annual meeting of the American Chemical Society in Washington, D.C. The symposium George proposes is to honor the contributions of Bob Eischens, who launched the research area of using infrared spectroscopy to study the adsorption of molecules on metals. This is an area in which both George and I have worked for the last thirty-five years. Such a symposium sounds interesting to me, and I ask who else is coming. "I don't know," says George, "You're the first person I called."

It is difficult to identify the absolute beginning of an idea. There is always some earlier event, something exerting an influence, moving you to that time that is temporarily the present. But in the case of my involvement in surface science, I can identify one of the beginnings precisely. As a graduate student I was doing my research under the supervision of Professor John Strong. For me the decision to work with John Strong was one of the better choices I have made. For my thesis research I explored new ways to spread the infrared spectrum into its component wavelengths (infrared interferometry) and ways to use stacks of thin, transparent layers, each of a precise thickness, to make filters that are useful in the infrared spectral region (infrared interference filters). In the course of this activity I learned about infrared spectroscopy.

Three decades earlier in the early 1930s, when infrared spectroscopy was in its infancy, it was an event in the scientific community when, for the first time, someone was able to record the infrared spectrum of water vapor, showing immediately that the water molecule is a bent molecule, with the oxygen atom in the middle and a hydrogen atom on each side; or the spectrum of carbon dioxide, unambiguously showing it to be a linear molecule with the carbon in the middle between two oxygen atoms; or that of nitrous oxide showing it to be a linear molecule, not symmetric like carbon dioxide, but asymmetric, of the form N-N-O. Considering the importance of these simple molecules to our world, the first unambiguous evidence of their structures, on the atomic scale, was a significant piece of fundamental knowledge. Had I been working then, I might have chosen to look into the structure of simple molecules.

But the field had changed. When I was a graduate student, infrared spectroscopists were studying the spectrum of infrared radiation that is emitted by hot matter or that is partially absorbed by gases or solids to learn about the structure of the emitting or absorbing material. Once the basic structure of the simple molecules was understood, spectroscopists were either looking at increasingly finer details in simple molecules or at the structure of more and more complicated molecules. It just wasn't to my taste to pursue that route as I was leaving graduate school. I preferred to be opening a new research field rather than helping refine a mature one. Since I had decided not to continue developing infrared interferometry, the subject of my thesis research, I was on the lookout for a new research area.

I had read something about molecules getting adsorbed on solid surfaces and the connections of this process with catalysis. A catalyst is a material that facilitates the reaction of two materials to form a new product. A common example is the process by which a vegetable oil is made to react with hydrogen (to become hydrogenated), which turns it into oleomargarine. The desired chemical reaction only takes place if a catalyst is present, but in the process the catalyst does not get used up. The supposition is that a molecule of one, or perhaps both, of the would-be reactants adsorbs on the surface of the catalyst, and in doing that changes its structure in some way that makes the molecules receptive to the reaction. After the reaction the newly produced molecule leaves the surface, which remains as it was before, ready to repeat the performance. The word catalyst has taken on a figurative meaning in the general vocabulary, referring to something that causes change to take place.

At that time the experiments performed in an attempt to understand these processes were what I call "black-box" experiments. By that I mean it was as if the system being studied were inside a black box, securely out of view of the investigator, who could only change the mixture of things that were put into the box and observe how that changed the mixture of things that came out. What was needed was some way to look inside the box at the processes that were taking place. It seemed clear that the crucial step in the catalytic process lay in the details of what happened to a molecule when it was adsorbed, and there, it seemed to me, might be a new and fruitful application of infrared spectroscopy.

The adsorbed molecules have bonds to atoms on the surface and, in a sense, this adsorbed layer constitutes a new kind of matter that doesn't exist anywhere, except at the surface of the solid. If one could record the infrared spectrum of these molecules while they are adsorbed on the surface, then he or she might be able to determine their structure. The effect of such a new tool would be to take the problem of catalysis out of the black box, examining the crucial adsorption step by a much more direct method. It seemed like a good idea, but it was in a field about which I knew very little.

I described the idea to John Strong, who said that although he himself didn't know anything about adsorption and catalysis, Paul Emmett, in the Chemistry Department on the Johns Hopkins campus, was one of the world's experts in this area. He suggested that I talk with Paul Emmett about the idea. A few days later I knocked on Professor Emmett's door and asked if I might talk with him. The level of my self-confidence was rather low as I approached a world expert to ask questions in an area where my ignorance was nearly complete. He said that he was just getting ready to leave to attend a Gordon Conference on catalysis (I'll discuss the Gordon Conferences shortly), but he could talk with me if I didn't mind him wandering around and gathering up some things from his office while we talked.

I agreed and started to propose the idea that it might be interesting to deposit some porous layer of an infrared-transparent material and then adsorb a gas to cover the large surface area of the pores. The spectrum of the infrared light transmitted through the porous layer would show the absorption spectrum of the adsorbed molecules, and by studying it, we might learn something about how the molecules were bound to the surface.

I still have a mental snapshot of Professor Emmett's reaction to my suggestion. He was reaching to get a book off an upper shelf, and he turned to me, his outstretched hand on the book, and said sharply, "Where did you get this idea?" It sounded to me as if he had caught me with my hand in the cash drawer. I was confused at his sharp question. My answer was a mumbled response to the effect that I really didn't know anything about this area . . . it just seemed as if it might be a good idea . . . but I really didn't know. . . .

The reason for his question became clear when he told me that a short article had just appeared in the *Journal of Chemical Physics* by Eischens, Pliskin, and Francis in which they reported recording the infrared spectrum of carbon monoxide adsorbed on very small metal particles. He thought it looked like a very promising approach to the study of adsorption and was thinking of starting some similar work. His question was not accusatory, as I had thought, but he was wondering, naturally enough, whether my suggestion was prompted by this recent article. I had not seen the article.

My involvement with this new field had to wait for three years after that conversation until I finished my degree, moved, and started a new job in 1957. At that time there was a shortage of people with degrees in physics, and there were many job opportunities in both academia and industry. I decided to work in industry, thinking that, although I would like to go to a university eventually, it would be good to first have the experience of an industrial laboratory.

That decision was made in a very different context than exists today. Following World War II there was an attitude toward basic research that persisted up to the late 1960s, which was a faith that basic research was the key to new products. Quite a number of large companies had basic research laboratories in which scientists were given a relatively free hand to choose the work they pursued. Different laboratories required different degrees of relevance to the company's area of technology and also had different expectations of how much responsibility the scientist would take to help with problems that came up in the course of the company's business. However, a career in basic research within an industrial laboratory seemed a realistic possibility.

Before I went job hunting, I formulated a research plan that used infrared spectroscopy to investigate adsorbed molecules. When, in a job interview, we got to a discussion of the kind of basic research that might be supported, I asked very specifically if this were an area the laboratory would be willing to support. At the General Electric research laboratories in Schenectady they were willing to let me work half-time on this project and half-time on projects of more immediate interest to the company; at the Allis Chalmers research laboratory in Milwaukee they were willing to have me work full time on the project I proposed.

In the past twenty years Allis Chalmers has disappeared from view, but even in 1957 it seemed to many a strange choice. In the consumer market the company was best known for its manufacture of farm tractors and implements, not an area that one might think would prosper with the infusion of undirected research activity. However, the company was also involved in large electric power generators, transformers, electrical switching gear, turbines for driving generators, and a wide variety of equipment to do everything from processing mined ores to making breakfast cereals. The "concentration" of the central research laboratory was to investigate processes that had some connection with energy generation, distribution, application, and conversion from one form to another. It is easy to connect almost any area in physics to the conversion of energy into different forms; when I made that connection with my proposed project, the laboratory agreed to hire me and support my research.

So I started in a research area that was new to me, in a laboratory where there were no other persons with a specific interest or background in that area. Looking back on the decision, I see that it has several earmarks of a dumb move. Today I would advise a student of mine who is contemplating such a venture, which involves moving into an unfamiliar research field, to spend a year or two as a postdoc in a lab where similar work is done and pick up some background in ideas and techniques. At the time, however, all I was asking of an employer was to give me a salary and the freedom to work on a project of my own choosing, a project that appeared to me to have prospects for producing good science.

The laboratory gave me a great deal of freedom. Partly because of the isolation of my work, I made progress slowly. I intentionally involved myself in a few projects of more direct interest to the company and took upon myself the job of keeping an eye out in my reading of the scientific literature for new developments that might be of importance to others in the company. It seemed to me that the company was missing an important contribution from its basic researchers by not asking them to serve this lookout function for relevant new developments. On one occasion I set up a demonstration of a new optical device that seemed to have an application to problems faced by engineers in various parts of the company. As far as I know, none of these efforts finally yielded any benefit to Allis Chalmers.

I published a few papers on other topics, but it took about three years until I thought I had unraveled the story of the changes that take place when a molecule of methyl or ethyl alcohol adsorbs on the surface of aluminum oxide. I wrote the paper for submission to a scientific journal, but I had some qualms about mailing it. It was an interpretation in an area where all of my "expertise" was home-grown, and I knew how easy it is to miss something obvious when you don't have anyone to look at your work with a critical eye.

So we hired John Overend, an infrared spectroscopist from the University of Minnesota, to come as a consultant and spend a day considering the work and the manuscript describing it. When he failed to come up with any serious flaws in the interpretation, I felt reassured and submitted the paper. The paper was published and became a rather frequently quoted model for adsorption on metal oxides. Some years later it was included in a reprint collection of *Significant Papers on Catalysis*.

When I started working at Allis Chalmers, I considered it a way I could work on some basic research problems that interested me. That the company also thought it was in their interest to have me do this work made it a satisfactory arrangement. I did take on a few projects that seemed relevant to the company's more immediate interests, but the community that I identified with was the international scientific community. It came as something of a surprise to me to realize after two or three years that it did indeed matter to me what my reputation was within the company.

I started out thinking that I would ask no more than a salary and support to do my work, but I had the growing realization that I wanted to be considered a contributing citizen in the community where I worked. If I had the conviction that the work I was doing was, in fact, in the long-term interest of the company, then I should have been satisfied to do a good job at it. But it seemed to me that there were a number of instances where the company should have called on the expertise of the people in the central research labs but showed little interest in our work. I began to think about the next step, which was either to leave the lab or, if I stayed, to direct my work more closely to the solution of problems that would be valued by the company. After five years at Allis Chalmers, I decided it was time to move on.

I chose to go to a university and made the move in 1962. The collapse of the central research laboratory at Allis Chalmers didn't take place for another five years. However, even before I left, I began to see signs of impatience with the slow trickle of results from the laboratory. Where was this flow of products that was supposed to come from undirected fundamental research and boost the fortunes of the company? There were a couple of big development projects prematurely launched on too-tentative research results. My disillusionment with the benefits of unmanaged basic research matured, until the company wiped out the entire lab and went out of the basic-research business. Allis Chalmers was not alone; the same scenario was played out in many medium- and large-sized companies throughout the country.

When the lab closed, I felt sad, considering the great waste of resources that it represented. In hindsight it seemed clear to me that with better research management, the company could have been left with a viable basic-research group. Successful management would mean identifying areas in which the company could capitalize on new information but, within this area, give some freedom to motivated researchers to choose the direction of their investigations. Those are the thoughts of hindsight; when I was in it, I had no more vision of the trends than, apparently, anyone else.

In a sense these were moot points, because Allis Chalmers also had other problems. It would seem to me to make an interesting case study in industrial mismanagement to follow the steps by which an old-time, well-diversified company with a good reputation for high-quality products could, in one decade, be run into bankruptcy and disappear from the scene, which happened a few years after the research labs were closed. I did not anticipate any of these developments but left because I felt that the university was the place where I really wanted to be.

As I was making the transition, a meeting was being organized that would influence the development of my research career. There are many methods of communication among working scientists. In addition to books and scientific journals there are meetings where scientists get together to present their results and find out what their colleagues have learned. The Gordon Research Conferences are a group of meetings that have been operating for several decades and have become an institution in the scientific community. The Conferences are a collection of meetings organized under a set of rules designed to maximize the informal exchange of information between scientists working in a common field.

Typically a group of about one hundred scientists, all actively working in the same area, will gather in a somewhat isolated location, such as a college campus in a small New England town. The effect of the location is to encourage the participants to spend their leisure time together, and the organizers, who see the importance of such contact, insist that there be considerable unscheduled time in the week-long meeting. To encourage people to talk freely about their work in progress, where conclusions may still be tentative, the rule is that there are to be no published proceedings from the meetings, and discussions at the meetings may not be cited as sources in published papers.

A Gordon Conference on Catalysis has been meeting in alternate years for a long time. Keith Hall, from the Mellon Institute in Pittsburgh, was elected to organize the conference that would meet in the summer of 1963. He was aware of the small but increasing number of papers that reported efforts to understand the structure of adsorbed molecules by the application of infrared spectroscopy, and he decided it was time for the community of catalytic chemists to take a look at this new field to see if it were anything they ought to consider. At his invitation most of the people in the world who had published in the new area attended that meeting. Of course, Bob Eischens, whose work had stimulated much of the activity (and whose continuing work stimulated the special symposium at the American Chemical Society meeting in Washington, D.C., thirty-one years later), was there.

Most of the people attending the meeting, unlike me, came from a background of chemistry. When I gave a short report on my work, describing what happened to an alcohol molecule as it adsorbed on the surface of aluminum oxide, I felt as if I were standing naked in front of that group. Someone commented, "Everyone knows that when alcohol adsorbs on alumina (such-and-such) happens, and yet you are saying that (something else) takes place. How do you explain that?" I could only say that I didn't have much background in these matters, but here was the evidence for my interpretation.

Some years later, following one of my talks, someone in the audience asked how it felt to be a physicist talking to an audience of chemists. I replied that if my ego strength were high enough, I would say that I felt like a lion in a den of Daniels. (The answer was greeted by the appropriate chorus of hisses, boos, and laughter.) But at this first Gordon Conference, where I felt intimidated by people who knew so much more that I, such a comment would have been the farthest thing from my mind.

That Conference was suffused with the excitement of enthusiasts coming together for the first time. I still have contact with a number of the people whom I met there. I met Norman Sheppard, with whom I later spent a year at the University of East Anglia in Norwich, England. Les Little from the University of Western Australia has spent several months working in my lab, and I have visited him at Perth. Two people, Keith Hall, the organizer, and Jose Fripiat, from Belgium, later became faculty members in the chemistry department of my university. And when, thirty-one years later, the symposium was organized in honor of the contributions made by Bob Eischens, a significant number of the people from that 1963 Gordon Conference participated.

When I decided to leave Allis Chalmers, Barbara and I assumed that we would be leaving Milwaukee. I went to talk with Julian Mack, a senior physics faculty member at the University of Wisconsin in Madison, whom I had known from my work in infrared interferometry. I had a high regard for him, both as a scientist and as a person. I asked if he knew of any open positions in physics departments in the country. He said that it appeared to him that there were going to be some very interesting developments on the Milwaukee campus, and he urged me to talk to the chairman of the department there.

The University of Wisconsin-Milwaukee campus had been established six years before by the combination of two existing institutions, a University Extension Division and a State Teachers College, and was proclaimed to be the beginning of the second campus of the University of Wisconsin. Despite the rhetoric, which included some references to "separate, but equal, campuses," it had largely remained an undergraduate teaching institution and not a likely place where I might pursue a research and teaching career. Julian Mack correctly interpreted my non-committal reply to his suggestion as indicating that I had no intention of considering Milwaukee, so he rephrased his recommendation: "In fact, I would consider it a personal favor to me if you would talk with Mike Shurman there." As a personal favor to Julian I would have done many things, and so I called Mike Shurman.

Things were indeed changing in the University of Wisconsin System. The president of the University had unexpectedly died, and his successor, from within the University, Fred Harrington, was a person popular with the faculty, the Board of Regents, and the state legislature. One of his first orders of business was to spell out his plan of what should happen on the Milwaukee campus. He proposed that it be developed into a major university campus located in the urban population center of Wisconsin. It was to develop research areas and graduate programs and be essentially autonomous from its prestigious sister institution in Madison. He secured agreement with this plan from the Board of Regents and the state government, and the stage was set for change at Milwaukee.

I see now that this path was not unique but followed in a number of states, where a second campus was developed during the times when universities were bursting their seams, trying to accommodate the college population of the post-World War II baby boom. Some of those campuses developed more successfully than others, depending on the timing of their inception, levels of support, and leadership. The expanded role in graduate education of some of those campuses will survive—and some will not survive—the budget crises of state governments in the last decade of this century and the first decade of the next.

The main thing that the Milwaukee campus had to offer me was the promise of a chance to build. The Physics Department research tradition extended into the past for all of one year, starting with the hiring of Bill Walters, who had a nuclear physics background and ambitions to establish a research laboratory. He broke new ground in such basic ways as helping the financial managers set up accounts so that he could be reimbursed for copper tubing and pipe fittings, needed for laboratory apparatus, with funds that were labeled "research."

I listened very carefully to older members of the department to pick up signs of their resentment at this new activity, but I didn't hear any; I only heard people who took pride in the fact that Bill was really getting some research started. They were not going to be involved in research themselves but were supportive of those of us who did want to be involved.

This was not the attitude in all departments. It was understandable that some people resented the change. They had joined the faculty on this campus counting on a career in undergraduate teaching, and Fred Harrington's new vision of the role of this campus brought a change in the expectations of what would constitute a successful career at this institution. In some departments there were groups that dug in their heels, resisting the transformation at every step, for example, in decisions on hiring, salary recommendation, promotion, and the use of department resources. To this day I can see traces in some departments of the contention caused by that abrupt change in the ground rules.

The Physics Department was quite free of this strife. Still, without Bill Walters' presence I would not have taken the gamble of coming to this institution. I decided to risk it—and indeed the move was a gamble for someone with hopes of a research career.

Was this another dumb move? It was the second time I had moved to an environment where there was no group interested in my chosen area of research. If I count such things as the establishment of my "laboratory" with the orange crates, next to the barn in West Unity, the number was higher. Maybe there was an unconscious pattern in my decisions. This time, however, I would take an active role in developing the environment in which I would work for the next thirty-five years.

A lot of things had to be done if Fred Harrington's vision were to be implemented. Functions that had been handled, reluctantly, by departmental committees or subcommittees at Madison had to move to our new campus. The University of Wisconsin has a long tradition of strong faculty involvement in matters of governance. I believe that overall this tradition has good effects on the institution, but it has its price: you can only have faculty involvement in decisions if you have faculty willing to spend the necessary time to help make the decisions.

For the next nine years, while pursuing my research and teaching activities and helping to develop the department, I found myself on almost every major committee in the University, helping develop the infrastructure of the new institution. The committee route provides relevant experience if one is heading toward a career in academic administration, but it is a strategic mistake if one is trying to optimize a research career. A chance observation in my early years at the University, however, gave me some insight into what I was really doing.

At scientific meetings I would run into friends from graduate school or other contemporaries who had also opted for positions in Universities, and we would talk about how things were going in our professional lives. It came as a shock to me during one of these conversations to realize that while my friends were talking about the people running the departments and the universities as "they" and the policies as "what they are trying to do," I was referring to the people running the department and the university as "we." It was totally unconscious, but I think it revealed a significant commitment I had made. I felt that it was my university and I was trying to make it a good place to be. Bill Walters was a partner in this effort.

Bill and I had come from quite different backgrounds in physics, but we had both been attracted by some interesting problems having to do with processes that take place at surfaces. Bill had become aware of effects that take place in the vacuum chambers of particle accelerators. When electrons or other charged particles strike the vacuum-chamber walls, a variety of particles, some with positive charges, some with negative charges, and some neutral—with no charge—are emitted. In an accelerator these processes are impediments to maintaining a good vacuum, but the processes are interesting in and of themselves, and Bill had obtained some equipment to investigate such effects in his lab in Milwaukee. I had decided to make a serious attempt to see if I could develop the reflection method of studying adsorbed molecules on an extended metal surface.

At a few laboratories around the country researchers were involved in investigations, some called surface chemistry and some called surface physics, but most of these investigations used the "black-box" approach. A few new techniques, however, promised to give a description of surface processes in molecular or atomic terms. The work was scattered.

In a physics department a person analyzed patterns produced on a fluorescent screen by slow-moving electrons that bounced back when they hit a metal crystal. It was found that patterns could be interpreted to reveal details of the arrangement of atoms on the surface and also of the arrangement of a layer of molecules adsorbed on the surface. In a chemistry department a person was using infrared spectroscopy to try to understand the role of adsorbed molecules in catalysis. In an electrical engineering department a person was looking at Auger (pronounced o-ZHAY) electrons emitted from surface atoms when they were bombarded by a beam of fast-moving electrons. By analyzing the energies of the emitted electrons, he could not only detect the presence of very small numbers of adsorbed atoms but also see differences, depending on how they were bound to the surface.

These were all techniques for getting a new kind of atomic-level information from the surface, but they were being used by people from different disciplines who described their results using the language peculiar to their own disciplines, published their findings in different journals, attended different scientific meetings, and, in general, had little contact with one another. In 1963 Bill and I began to develop the conviction that there was a new research area here, about to emerge. It obviously should develop as an interdisciplinary effort involving people from physics, chemistry, and engineering, and it was an ideal area for an emerging institution such as ours to develop.

It took a couple of years to formulate the plans and convince people in the concerned departments and in the administration that this was an area that would develop rapidly and become a productive and important activity over the next few decades. In February 1966 we had a conference to which we invited a number of people involved or interested in this kind of research. We described our plans for an interdisciplinary laboratory and asked advice on what areas should be included. We hired five of the people who attended that meeting, and with the four already present, we launched the Laboratory for Surface Studies.

It is very satisfying to see that the claims we made about the development of this scientific area—predictions that we were convinced must be correct—turned out, in fact, to be correct. Our Laboratory for Surface Studies became the first of a number of laboratories, institutes, centers, and departments at academic institutions and industrial labs around the world to develop this new approach to a wide variety of surface problems.

There was an important element to the success of this endeavor that I did not understand until later. While trying to develop the plan for this interdisciplinary laboratory, I talked with a number of people who had more experience than I and whose judgment I respected. From more than one of them I got a response something like this:

"Interdisciplinary groups tend to be very fragile. They are unstable and tend to be taken over by one or another of the disciplines involved. It is easy to set up an interdisciplinary group on paper, but it is difficult to make it a functioning reality. If you have Professor A in Department 1 who wants to work with Professor B in Department 2, then you have an interdisciplinary activity; without that combination, you do not."

I was puzzled by the cautious attitude of some of these people toward what, to me, was so clearly a wonderful plan. Later I came to appreciate that what they told me was absolutely correct. You can find organizational skeletons at many institutions where interdisciplinary activities have either become monodisciplinary or have evolved into separate groups existing under the organizational umbrella but having little creative interaction with each other. Fortunately, circumstances peculiar to our situation at the University of Wisconsin-Milwaukee in the 1960s helped us avoid that fate.

It is very difficult to organize an interdisciplinary activity by decisions made from above, particularly in a university setting where faculty autonomy is so highly prized. However, we were not starting with a group of people whose habits of association needed to be changed. In an era when there was a shortage of new faculty members, the major attraction we had to a prospective faculty member was our plan for the future.

There is a real benefit in talking about a subject of mutual interest with a person who has a background different from yours. You use different language to describe physical phenomena and different starting places in trying to understand a new effect, and you approach a problem with different reservoirs of understanding. It is not a matter of one way being better than the other; two ways of considering a problem are likely to suggest a third, involving insight deeper than either of the others.

But this benefit comes at a considerable cost. As I stood before the chemists at that Gordon Conference on Catalysis, I was in the situation of not knowing simple things that any graduate student in chemistry would know. I was off my home turf and feeling very vulnerable to being put down for my ignorance in matters well known to this group. In such a situation nothing good is going to happen unless both groups are willing to ask—and to patiently answer—what might be considered to be stupid questions. For people with different backgrounds to benefit from that difference, they have to have a certain degree of humility.

The only people who were attracted to our plan for an interdisciplinary laboratory in the 1960s were those who were already convinced that the benefits of associating with people from other backgrounds were worth the effort and discomfort that it required. We selectively hired only those who were already convinced of the value of the approach; without that conviction, there was little reason for them to want to come to this new institution.

We made the decision that each person associated with the Laboratory for Surface Studies would have one of the departments as his or her academic home. This meant that the department had to approve the hiring of the faculty member, and the department controlled the tenure decisions. This has not been a problem in general because we have been fortunate to attract very good people to our Laboratory. One of the resulting problems of the Laboratory, however, has been the high attrition that has come from members being tapped for administrative jobs in the University. According to my count the Laboratory for Surface Studies, which has typically had about fifteen members, has provided, at different times, eight department heads, four associate deans for science in the college of Letters and Science, two deans of the graduate school, and two vice chancellors.

We intentionally left the details of the organization of the Laboratory for Surface Studies open until we had hired a critical mass of faculty, so that we could involve them in designing their (our) own environment. When, in the early days of the Laboratory, we applied for a grant from the National Science Foundation to help support the development, we were visited by a team of scientists sent to help NSF evaluate our proposal. As they were ready to leave, one of the visitors commented that he had seen groups with a strong interdisciplinary organization on paper that had no real cooperative activity going on, but he had never before seen such a strong interdisciplinary group in practice that had so little organization on paper.

As the group grew, the weekly Surface Studies Seminar became a very important part of the Laboratory. With some hindsight I see that it was an absolutely essential part of the activity. Although the visiting speakers helped keep us and our students connected with the international community, the most critical talks were those of our own faculty and students, describing their current efforts. People who were a part of the Laboratory were housed in three separate buildings. It was in the seminar that we found out what was going on in those other buildings, or, in fact, in our own buildings, and became involved in the design of the experiments and the interpretation of the data. Without that regular contact it would have been easy for the interdisciplinary activity to slip away. This regular contact is still something that needs to be watched and nurtured. It is easy to think that talks by visiting scientists are more important than those of our own graduate students. If the visitors are not appropriately briefed, however, they may give their talks assuming a very specialized audience, and we find that more of the chemistry members are showing up for talks given by chemists and more physicists come for talks by physicists. And without our own students talking about their work, we lose track of what is going on next door. Some of the people with whom I originally discussed the idea of an interdisciplinary surface studies group were absolutely correct. Real interdisciplinary activities are fragile and can disappear unless they are carefully tended.

There are two different kinds of organizations that might be described as interdisciplinary groups. In one, a large project is undertaken by a group where the contribution from each member is agreed upon and organizational effort is directed to keeping all the individuals working smoothly together. I have never been a part of such a group and, while it is, no doubt, the appropriate approach for some large projects, it is not attractive to me personally.

For example, when I was an undergraduate at the University of Rochester, that institution had a cyclotron that was, for a brief period of time, one of the largest in the world. I was greatly impressed by the magnitude of the project, and although it was an exciting development, I could see that it was not the kind of research that I would most like to be involved in. The process of doing an experiment involved planning and scheduling the efforts of a large team of people, each a specialist in one part of this vast, complicated apparatus. Even at that time, when I had not been involved in any research, I thought that I would prefer to work on a project where I could understand all of the parts myself and make my own decisions about what to do next—and when to do it.

This has been true throughout my research career: I want to be able to follow my own hunches (and make my own mistakes) without having to convince others that it is the best way to go. I'm not condemning the large group approach; for some large projects I assume that it is the only effective approach. My attitude is an aesthetic judgment of how I like to work.

However, on the national scale, when we make decisions as to how to support basic research in the country, the issue becomes something more than a question of personal taste. It becomes a debate on how far we should go in spending the available research money on "Big Science," a few large projects that must involve teams of researchers working together, rather than on "Little Science," small projects organized around individuals following their own hunches and enthusiasms. I believe that Little Science yields large returns for the research dollar, and we make a mistake to sacrifice it for large, expensive, highly visible group projects. But this is a digression from my story about our development of our Laboratory for Surface Studies in Milwaukee.

The laboratory we envisioned was the second of the two kinds of interdisciplinary groups. It involved a collection of people with some common interests, educating and stimulating each other, but each running his or her own show. Joint projects would arise as people chose to work together on projects of mutual interest. Coauthors from different departments appearing together on published papers would give evidence of such successful collaborations. But in this kind of interdisciplinary group the scientific output relies on the effort and ingenuity of individuals. Let me describe the path of my individual effort.

Some very interesting results had come from the infrared study of adsorption on small metal particles, but one of the problems with that method was that we knew very little about the nature of the surface of these tiny crystals, only about twenty or thirty atoms in diameter. A number of the new techniques being developed could get amazingly detailed information about the organization of the atoms on the surface of a metal crystal. The samples used for such investigations were single metal crystals, perhaps a quarter of an inch in diameter, that could be cut and polished to expose a particular crystal face. If we could get the infrared spectrum of molecules adsorbed on such a surface, then we could combine the infrared information with the results of several others of these new techniques. Each technique provides a different insight into what is happening at the surface, and the combination could produce a detailed picture that would be beyond the capabilities of any one of the techniques.

I went back to try again to do the calculation that I had not been able to do with the computing facility at Allis Chalmers. I wanted to calculate the reflectance of an infrared beam from an extended metal surface and see how it would be affected by a layer of adsorbed molecules. In particular, I wanted to know what to expect if I looked at the spectrum of the infrared beam reflected from the surface. If the molecules on the surface absorbed a band of infrared wavelengths, how big a dip would show in the spectrum of the reflected light? This was the fundamental question that would determine whether or not the experiment was feasible. With the aid of a computer this time my students and I were able do the calculation.

The results told us that we didn't have a chance in the world of "seeing" a single layer of adsorbed molecules (a monolayer) unless we did the experiment in just the right way. The beam would have to be reflected at a very high angle, almost grazing the surface. At this optimum angle the dip in the spectrum of the reflected infrared beam would be five thousand times greater than if we reflected the beam straight back from the surface.

This was a crucial result, because even at the optimum angle it appeared to be a borderline experiment. There were several approximations in the calculation, and my conclusion was that maybe it would work and maybe it wouldn't, and we would have to do the experiment very carefully to see which was the reality. I published the results of the first calculation and, while getting funds for a new infrared spectrometer and building the appropriate system to do the experiment, continued to do more calculations of how to optimize the experiment.

We hoped that we would be able to detect the infrared spectrum of a monolayer of adsorbed molecules, that is, a layer of adsorbed molecules only one molecule thick, so that each molecule is bonded directly to the atoms in the metal surface. It turned out that with the spectrometers available at the time, when the experiment was done very carefully, we were able to do better than that: we could detect the spectrum of fewer molecules than those that constituted a monolayer. We could actually study molecules present in a concentration as low as a few percent of a monolayer. To this day I am pleased and surprised with that result.

John Pritchard and his student, Alex Bradshaw, at Queen Mary College in London, were the first to successfully do the experiment, following the experimental method suggested by my calculation. I later worked with

Alex when he was a Director at the Fritz Haber Institute in Berlin.

A student, Harland Tompkins, was the first in my lab to demonstrate the success of the approach by obtaining the spectrum of carbon monoxide adsorbed on a copper film and on a gold film. Later another student, Juan Carlos Campuzano, combined the infrared technique with several others, all in the same vacuum system, and was able to describe in considerable detail the way carbon monoxide molecules adsorbed on the surface of a single nickel crystal. For example, he could tell that starting with a clean surface, the carbon monoxide molecules would move on the nickel surface to come to rest in positions where they would contact three nickel atoms. As more molecules were adsorbed, and the surface began to get a bit crowded, they all shifted to a different crystal site—to a location where they each contacted only two nickel surface atoms. At yet higher coverage a beautifully symmetric, repeating arrangement of the adsorbed molecules developed, with some contacting two atoms and some only a single atom in the surface of the nickel crystal.

Our technique, used together with other techniques, was succeeding in yielding the kind of detailed information about adsorption that we had hoped for. We, and many others, working with the new tools available to surface scientists, had succeeded in taking the adsorption and catalytic investigations of fifteen years ago out of their "black boxes."

For a few years John Pritchard and I, with our students, were the only ones working in this area. Both of us had relatively small research groups. We operated our labs with limited resources and made progress rather slowly. If an obviously good experiment couldn't get done this year, perhaps it would get done the next. In the early 1970s a few other people started to use this infrared reflection-absorption technique, combined in the same apparatus with other techniques, to get detailed information about the process of adsorption.

By the latter half of the decade the field had changed drastically. Additional new techniques were developed to probe the vibrations of molecules adsorbed on metal surfaces, and theoretical chemists and physicists "discovered" the field. What they discovered was that here was a developing body of reliable experimental information ready to be incorporated into theoretical models that described, in more and more complete terms, what happens when molecules interact with a surface. Large laboratories, with more resources than John or I had, joined the game, and the obviously good experiments got picked off at a rapid rate. The developments clearly marked a successful maturing of the field, but it was no longer "my" field.

Rich McQuistan, one of the early members of the Laboratory, did experimental research work until he had to give it up when he was tapped for administrative posts. He did continue, even through his term as the Dean of the Graduate School—aided by the use of much midnight oil—with theoretical research and produced a continual flow of research papers. I remember a casual conversation we had at one time about the fantasies we held about our research careers. It was surprising to find that his image and mine were very different. Rich could imagine a successful career in which he completely developed, by his own efforts, an entire research area.

"I would open a new area," he said, "and just mine it clean."

I replied, "If I could operate any way I wanted to, I would be a successful dilettante. I would do a few experiments to open up a new research area and develop an indication of its scientific potential and then, when all of the 'serious' workers moved in, move to open up another new field."

It is interesting to see how those fantasies actually shaped our careers. Rich developed mathematical methods for counting the number of different ways a certain number of particles could be arranged at the sites of a square lattice. The work was stimulated by problems concerning adsorbed molecules on a crystal surface. The mathematics got more and more sophisticated as he tackled more and more difficult problems. Instead of single particles, how about dumbbells (two particles fastened together that would occupy two adjacent lattice sites)? or N-bells (N particles fastened together in a straight line)? or non-linear N-bells?

He solved a long series of successively more difficult and more general problems that lie in a general theoretical field called statistical mechanics. He realized that his results had application, not only to adsorption of molecules on surfaces but to problems in crystal growth, magnetism, heat capacities, and a variety of esoteric topics that are seldom mentioned on the evening news. Recorded in the scientific literature is a research area in which most of the results are his. For several years I urged him to bring all the pieces he developed together in a book, but the siren call of yet one more case, or one more application, has kept him from the book.

A number of the decisions that I have made are consistent with my fantasy. When the method of reflection-absorption infrared spectroscopy became more widely used, it seemed to me to be time to move on. As more and more of the adsorption arrangements of simple molecules on simple crystal surfaces were solved, people started looking at more complicated systems. They began to investigate the simultaneous adsorption of more than one kind of molecule on the surface, or to look at adsorption on an alloy where the surface contained more that one kind of metal atom, or to look at the adsorption of complicated molecules.

Some of these approaches are prompted by real-world problems and are good problems to work on. But the more complicated problems are not to my taste, and I do not like to be just one more person working in an area where others are equipped to be more productive than I. So I decided to shift my attention to two different sets of problems. I can describe one of the problems best if I first discuss a different experimental approach that was developed during the 70s.

Another technique had been developed that could determine the natural vibration frequencies of adsorbed molecules. Instead of reflecting an infrared beam from a surface, one could bounce a beam of electrons off the surface and, by studying the amounts of energy lost by the electrons, could deduce the vibrational frequencies of the adsorbed molecules. This method, called electron energy-loss spectroscopy, gives information similar to that obtained from the infrared technique, but with some advantages and some disadvantages. For example, the electron method has good sensitivity and can yield a spectrum over a very wide range in a short time. However, the infrared method yields much higher resolution; it can separate two absorption bands so close together that the electron method would see them as only one broad band. Each technique could solve some problems that the other could not.

One of the common beliefs, shared by most of those who compared these two techniques, was that, unlike the electron method, the infrared method could not be used to look at the low-frequency vibrations of molecules. I had the feeling that this was not a fundamental limitation; if we solved some technical problems and really did the experiment right, we could bring the advantages of the infrared method to this low-frequency region.

Xiao-Dong (Larry) Wang took on the problem as a graduate student and, after a long, hard struggle with our aging spectrometer, was able to work in this region and show the existence of three different forms of oxygen adsorbed on a silver surface. The results were significant both for the information about the oxygen-silver system (a system of considerable commercial importance) and as a demonstration that the advantages of this infrared method could reasonably be applied to the entire infrared spectral region.

We were not the first to produce results in this region. By the time we published our results, three other groups had produced some results in the low-frequency part of the infrared spectrum. They had used considerably more sophisticated equipment than we had: a synchrotron light source, superconducting detectors, and a new generation of infrared spectrometers. We concluded that this spectral region was "open for business as usual."

The other area to which we turned our attention may seem like a great leap backward. We decided to look again at adsorption on the kind of small metal particles that Bob Eischens initially used to stimulate this whole enterprise. What kind of regressive behavior was this? Actually, although the experiments appeared to be similar to earlier ones of Eischens, we were now looking at these systems with very different eyes from those we had before.

The combination of several techniques applied to the same extended-crystal samples had revealed details about the system of adsorbed molecules that we would never have known using only the infrared technique. Now we knew what was implied by an infrared band from adsorbed carbon monoxide occurring at a particular place in the spectrum. We knew how the interaction of adjacent, adsorbed molecules shifted the position of their infrared bands. In Berlin we had studied adsorption on crystal faces that had terraces of atoms across the surface and steps with zigzag edges, and we learned how the infrared spectrum of adsorbed carbon monoxide could tell us about the presence of these atoms at the edges of the steps. This was all preparation for looking at carbon monoxide adsorbed on tiny metal crystals where some of the atoms are located on edges, some on corners, and some on the small, flat crystal faces.

In some way the work had come full circle, returning to the problem that started it. As a student, Kurt Brandt took up the problem of applying all we had learned about the effects that influence the infrared spectrum of adsorbed carbon monoxide. His work shows the real possibility of being able to look at the spectrum of carbon monoxide adsorbed on some finely divided metal catalyst and tell a lot about the detailed nature of the metal surface. For example, it seems feasible to answer such questions as: What fraction of the atoms are in little flat crystal faces, and how big are those faces? How many of the metal atoms lie along edges of the crystal faces? How many sit on points?

The author with the infrared spectroscopy system built to study adsorbed molecules at Allis Chalmers Research Labs around 1960.

The author with a later surface-science apparatus at the University of Wisconsin-Milwaukee in 1992. *(Photo by Alan Magayne-Roshak)*

Suppose you were trying to understand why some metal, prepared in some special way, is a good catalyst for a particular reaction but is no good as a catalyst if prepared in a slightly different way. Wouldn't you think that if you could correlate these things with a detailed description of how the surfaces differ in the two cases, you might understand some significant things about the process? Yes, I would think so. With my retirement from this research area, however, the final application of the method will need to come from another laboratory.

I remained intimately involved with the Laboratory for Surface Studies, but Bill Walters took a different route. Bill is a person who does his homework. He is the one who, when the committee meets the second time, has looked up the information that was speculated on in the first meeting. The result of doing a good job in helping solve problems is to be given more jobs to do. In this new university Bill was quickly drafted into a variety of administrative jobs, ending with a ten-year term as Vice Chancellor before he came back to the Physics Department in 1981. I avoided moving into administration and continued to participate in the scientific activity of the Laboratory; without attention at that level the Laboratory would not develop. But Bill was in a position to promote the Laboratory at a different level.

Looking back, I think that this arrangement turned out to be good for the development of our interdisciplinary laboratory. My career has been enhanced by the presence of the Laboratory for Surface Studies. The Laboratory has prospered and has been a positive influence on its participating departments and, in many discernible ways, on the University.

> **Surface science has certainly been one of the continuing themes in my life. George is asking if I would like to be a part of a symposium honoring Bob Eischens and his contributions in this area. It seems to be an event celebrating a part of my culture. "Sure, George, I'll be there; I wouldn't miss it."**

Chapter Eleven

THE INFRARED RAINBOW

This morning's mail brings me a fat volume titled, *Selected Papers on Scattering in the Atmosphere*. It is one in a series described as "a reprint collection of outstanding papers from the world literature on optical and optoelectronic science, engineering, and technology," put together by Craig Bohren at Penn State. (Craig is another in the international community of sky nuts whose carefully written book on light scattering is the current starting place for anyone wanting to work in that area.) A quick look at the table of contents shows that of the fifty or so papers in the collection, he has included three of mine. Not bad. He has a long preface where he tries to justify the choices he had to make of "outstanding papers," and my attention is caught by a long paragraph where I spot the name Greenler in the first line:

> I chose Greenler's paper on the infrared rainbow in part because he told me that much to his surprise it has been the paper of his that has attracted the most attention and in part because of the following incident. Just before Thanksgiving last year one of my former students called me to ask, "Do you know about the infrared rainbow? I just heard something about it on the radio." My response was, "Of course, Greenler did something on it, but that was several years ago."

Within a few hours of this puzzling conversation, I went upstairs to take a bath. I brought my shortwave radio with me, tuned to the Voice of America Spanish-language broadcast, and turned on the water. As the water was flowing into the tub, the words *"arco iris infrarojo"* and *"el profesor Robert Greenler de la Universidad de Wisconsin en Milwaukee"* suddenly filtered through the noise of splashing water. I grabbed frantically for the taps, but by the time I got the water turned off the broadcaster had moved to another topic. This nearly simultaneous transmission of news of the infrared rainbow to a gringo in Washington, D.C., and Spanish-speaking people from Mexico to Tierra del Fuego was an omen I could not ignore.

That's great; the infrared rainbow surfaces once again!

There are several Thens to this Now. I had been interested in rainbows long before I had acquired the tools of the scientist with which to understand this marvelous arch of color, and I have been chasing rainbows all my life. But the idea of the infrared rainbow came to me about a quarter of a century before Bohren received his omen. Strangely enough, it was connected with my work in surface science.

It might seem that my interest in the structure of adsorbed molecules would have nothing to do with rainbows, but not so. Because I use infrared radiation to study adsorbed molecules, an understanding of the nature of infrared radiation is one of the tools of my scientific trade. Let me explain the relation of infrared radiation to the visible light by which we observe our world.

When we send white light through a prism, we spread it out into the spectrum that extends from violet on one end to red on the other. The physical difference between the violet and red light is that the waves that constitute the red light are longer than the waves of violet light. There are other waves, even longer, that constitute infrared "light." I put the word "light" in quotes when referring to the infrared waves, because we usually use that term to describe visible waves; the infrared waves are invisible. In one sense there is nothing strange about the infrared portion of the spectrum; it is very much like the blue or green or yellow or red light. The strange thing is that the human eye is only sensitive to a small part of the total spectrum, to that part that we call, naturally enough, the visible spectrum.

These two different strands of my experience, the rainbow and infrared radiation, came together one day while I was sitting at my desk, wool-gathering rather than addressing the task at hand. The question occurred to me: Could there be an infrared rainbow in the sky? It struck me as an interesting question, the interest perhaps enhanced by the circumstance that thinking about an infrared rainbow helped me avoid working on the project on my desk. How does one explore such a question? Here is the process I went through. For there to be an infrared rainbow:

1. *The source of light must emit infrared radiation.* The sun does emit in the infrared as well as in the visible part of the spectrum (and, in fact, over a much wider spectrum, from X-rays and ultraviolet rays to radio waves).

2. *The infrared radiation must pass through the Earth's atmosphere.* Water vapor, carbon dioxide, and other greenhouse gases absorb some infrared wavelengths, but others pass through unimpeded.

3. *A rainbow is formed by rays that enter a droplet of water and are reflected internally before emerging from the drop. So the infrared rays would have to pass through the water.* This is a serious consideration. Just because a droplet of water is transparent to visible light, we cannot assume that it is transparent to infrared "light." In fact, liquid water does absorb over a broad range of infrared wavelengths, but if we look at the measured infrared transmittance of water, we see that there is a band of wavelengths in the infrared, just beyond the red end of the spectrum, that also would be transmitted by a droplet of water.

4. *After emerging from the raindrop, the infrared rays that have passed all of these tests must again pass through the air to the unseeing eye of the would-be observer.*

This train of thought made the answer to the question clear: Yes indeed, there should be an invisible rainbow in the sky, lying just outside the red band of the visible bow. In searching the scientific literature, I could find no evidence that anyone had detected such a rainbow, and that made it seem to me to be an interesting quest. I decided to try to photograph it using an infrared-sensitive photographic film.

Left top: A photo from the first roll of film, recording the infrared rainbow in the spray of a leaky garden hose on top of a ladder.

Left bottom: A natural infrared rainbow, showing the primary bow with its supernumeraries, and the secondary bow.

Above: The photo used on the cover of the September 24, 1971, issue of *Science* that contained the short article on the infrared rainbow.

The problem in taking a picture with the infrared film is that it is sensitive not only to the infrared but to all of the visible light, and it is extremely sensitive to blue light. An exposure with this film would result in a black-and-white negative, but there would be no way to tell what part of the exposure was caused by what part of the spectrum. The key to sorting out that problem was a filter. I was able to get a filter that looked like a piece of black plastic, opaque to visible light but transparent to the infrared, just beyond the visible part of the spectrum. With this filter over the camera lens, and using the infrared film, any exposure that I obtained would result from invisible light.

Anyone who has tried to photograph rainbows knows that they usually occur when a camera is not at hand and fade just as one gets back with the camera. I decided to try an easier subject first, that of a rainbow formed in a water spray that I could turn on at my convenience in my back yard. I produced the water spray from a piece of hose with many small holes, mounted on top of a step ladder, and in that spray I photographed my first invisible rainbow.

That first roll of film yielded exciting results. Not only could I see the primary infrared bow, but also the secondary, and inside the primary there were the infrared supernumerary bows. Careful examination showed an additional, faint, very rare feature. There was a supernumerary on the outside of the secondary bow. For some subtle reasons this feature is not generally observed in photographs, and to this day this is one of the very few photographs that shows the effect.

After taking those photographs with the leaky-hose spray, I wanted to capture nature's own, natural, infrared rainbow. The usual problem existed: not having the camera at hand when the visible rainbow appeared. But the problem was compounded by needing not only the camera, but the infrared film, the filter, and the time to get them together before the bow disappeared. It was four more years until I, the camera, film, filter, and rainbow all came together at the same time, resulting in photos of a natural, invisible rainbow.

I submitted a short article to the journal *Science* with an additional photo that I suggested might be used for the cover picture. They published the article in 1971, using my photograph as the picture on the magazine cover for that issue. In some ways it was the simplest paper I ever published; it occupied only about a page, including a photo and a diagram. The article poses the question of whether an infrared rainbow exists and after a short description of the photographic arrangement concludes: Yes, it exists, and here is a photograph of it.

I probably received more mail concerning that brief note than any other paper I have published. Some were from people who had a scientific interest in the matter. Others were from friends, with whom ties had been stretched by distance and neglect, saying, "I'm glad to see that you're still at it." Other letters represented unique interests, such as the psychoanalyst studying color blindness, wondering whether such a disability might be a reason for my interest in invisible light and also speculating on the possible unconscious motivation in the name Greenler. A person from Belgium Television wanted photographs of the infrared rainbow for a show they were producing, insisting that they must be in color. But most of the letters were from people whose imagination had been tweaked by the idea of a real, but invisible, rainbow.

In 1984 an exhibition opened in the Science Museum in London titled, *Beyond Vision*. As described in the exhibition catalog, it consisted of ". . . one hundred historic scientific photographs—unique images revealing information otherwise inaccessible to the human eye. On all scales, from the submicroscopic to the cosmic, they expand our limited vision to reveal invisible radiations, vanishingly faint images, events imperceptibly swift or slow, or remote realms of space and ocean which we cannot see unaided. Each photograph in the exhibition has some special historic significance. Classics like Röntgen's X-ray of his wife's hand and the first colour view of a foetus inside the mother's womb share the stage with the discovery of planet Pluto and the earliest photographs of shock waves trailing a swift bullet."

The subjects of the exhibit were produced as a book by the same name, and there—amid the first color landscape of Mars, Muybridge's sequence of a running horse, Harold Edgerton's first photograph of a fish taken at a depth of 1600 meters, an 1847 photographic record of lightning, and the first optical pulsar—are two of my photographs of the invisible rainbow. In seeing that collection, I had the sense of traveling in pretty fast company.

The fashion in general physics textbooks in the past several years is to introduce into the text several one- or two-page essays on special topics. These are usually topics intended to add some interesting ideas or applications to catch the attention of a motivated student. At a scientific meeting Paul Tipler, the author of one of the widely used texts, asked if I would be willing to write an essay on rainbows for his upcoming third edition. I told him that I was leaving in a month for Malaysia, where I was going to be teaching for a year. Under the circumstances I wouldn't have the time to do it—unless he would happen to be interested in the infrared-rainbow story, which I could put together without too much work. He expressed some interest—but I didn't hear more about it and assumed that he had decided not to use it.

After I had been in Malaysia a few months, a fax message arrived from London addressed to "Professor Robert Greenler, somewhere in Malaysia." It was from an editor of Tipler's book who told me that the publisher wanted to include the rainbow essay and, of course, things were at a critical stage so that it was needed very soon. She would need the text of the essay, the rainbow photos, and a photo of me, soon, if she were to meet her publishing deadline.

I replied that her message in the bottle had washed up on the shores of the local fax machine and, although I was willing, there were some problems. The editor, living in London, was working with the publisher in New York City, and, although I was in Malaysia, the photographs that I would use were in my office in Milwaukee. We decided to give it a try; only the existence of the fax machine made it seem possible. I wrote the text and sent it to London for her editing. I sent a message to Kurt Brandt, a graduate student who had worked with me doing a master's thesis (and later a Ph.D. thesis), with a set of intricate instructions. ". . . in my office, look in the second drawer on the left side of that cabinet . . . if you find a folder labeled 'infrared rainbow,' see if you can locate a print of a picture which is the same as the one that appears in figure X of the paper that you might find if you look . . . and also find a copy of that graph . . . and if you don't find it there, look . . . and if you do find them, send them to this address in New York."

For a photo of myself I sent a snapshot taken on a beach in Malaysia, less formal, I'm sure, than they expected, but it was what was available. (Actually, I probably would have sent some similar photo even in other circumstances. I have always thought it unlikely for a student to identify him or herself with science when its practitioners are represented by formal portraits of famous old men.) Surprisingly enough, all the international pieces fit together, and the little essay appears in Tipler's third edition of *Physics for Scientists and Engineers*.

A version of the infrared-rainbow story has been translated into Polish and has appeared in the popular Polish physics magazine *Postepy Fiziki*, but the reincarnation of the story that prompted Craig's messages was a version published in *Optics News* titled "Beyond the (Visible) Rainbow." It was written as a story about the evolution of a small research project, from question to answer. It was picked up by a Washington, D.C., television station for a segment on a weekly science program, was on the radio, and was circulated through the media to, among other places, the Voice of America.

> So Craig's reaction is correct, there is nothing new with the infrared rainbow. It's just that whenever it gets mentioned in public, it attracts a little flurry of attention. Why? Who can predict what will catch people's fancy? Apparently there are a number of people in the world who share with me the fascination of "seeing" for the first time this bow, whose undetected presence in the sky predates that of a human consciousness on this planet.

Chapter Twelve

JUST PLAYING

The audience started the evening with an air of expectancy. They are responsive and appreciative toward what I am telling them about beautiful things they can see in the sky. I am showing them computer simulations of ice-crystal halos and arcs that mimic the photos so well that it is clear we have come up with the right explanation for these effects. The Golden Rondelle Theater in Racine is filled with people who are clearly glad to be here, and their enthusiasm feeds my own. There is an extended round of applause, and now it is time for questions. "Yes . . . there in the top row, in the far corner . . . ."

"Don't get me wrong—I'm not going to blow the whistle on you, or report you to our senator—but, really, there is no serious reason for your spending time on this stuff, is there? You're just doing this for your own amusement. Right?"

From this audience, that question, with its accusatory tone, is the last thing I expected. How on earth do I respond?

I had been asked essentially the same question before, with someone trying to find out whether this involvement with sky effects is a hobby or a part of my "work." But this time the question came across as an accusation, against which I was challenged to defend myself. "Who's paying for this? Is it really work or are you just playing?" In other circumstances it could be an interesting question.

At one time I put a fair amount of effort into bird photography. I adapted a war-surplus, aerial-reconnaissance lens to act as a long-focus, twenty-pound lens for my 35 mm camera, which I could use to photograph birds from a blind. My friend from Baltimore, Steve Simon, shared this interest, and we took similar kinds of photos, occasionally having them published in newspapers or magazines. But Steve was an ornithologist, and he used his photos in talks and classes. He got professional credit for his bird photography, whereas I did not. Later, when I became involved in photographing and understanding optical sky effects, I realized that I was in the same position as Steve had been with the bird photos. My interest in sky phenomena was not a professional duty, but I did get professional credit for my efforts

It is probably something of a chicken-and-egg question to ask whether my playing is influenced by my being a scientist, or whether I became a scientist because of the kinds of things I liked to play with. Without knowing which came first, I can think of a number of examples where there is a connection between my play and my work.

One of the summers when I was in college I had a job in Toledo, Ohio, and lived at home with my parents. On a Saturday afternoon I got the idea of sending up a hot-air balloon. To make the balloon, I pasted together a three-foot-diameter sphere of tissue paper and at the bottom formed a mouth with a ring of aluminum wire. The burner, which was to heat the air in the balloon, was a piece of alcohol-soaked cotton, wrapped in aluminum foil, held in the center of the ring by small wires.

Friends of my parents who came to visit that evening were intrigued as they saw me put the finishing touches on this balloon, and they wanted to see it launched. I had intended to fly it in the daytime but decided that I could as well launch it at night. So at ten o'clock that evening we drove out to a park that had some wide-open recreational fields to see how this creation would work. As soon as I lit the alcohol burner, the bag plumped into a rigid sphere, brightly illuminated from the internal flame. When released, it rose straight up, an impressive orange-glowing sphere in the dark night. It rose above the tree level of the nearby woods into a wind that moved it rapidly along—a magnificent sight as it swept away downwind.

But apparently, the flame was a bit too hot for the paper. I assume that the paper of the entire balloon was very hot, so that when it ignited, it burned almost instantaneously. I started to run to the distant spot where the balloon had disappeared to retrieve the ring and burner and was surprised when I came upon it, much closer than I expected. Apparently I had misjudged the distance of the balloon when it disappeared in a flash of light. Everyone present thought it a most impressive display and were delighted with the show.

It was not until the next day that I started to think of how that incident might have appeared to a person driving his car along the nearby road. What that person "saw with his very own eyes" depends entirely on his unconscious assumption of one factor—distance.

When you see an object near to you, your two-eyed vision gives you depth perception that tells you how far away it is. If it is a familiar object whose size you know, then the size also gives you a sense of its distance. For example, the size effect will enable you to judge that a car is one hundred feet or one thousand feet away, even though at these distances your binocular vision provides no depth perception.

When you view an unfamiliar object in a situation where you have no other distance clues, you may have some impression of its distance, but this is tied, frequently, to an unconscious judgment of how big it is. For example, suppose that you see a strange sphere in the sky, of a size so that it just covers the full moon. You would probably not assume that it is as big as the moon. In fact, by looking at the moon itself, you have no real impression of how big it is. In a case like this, for a distant object where your binocular vision gives you no distance clues, the only information you really have is the "angular diameter" of the object.

You could measure the angular diameter of the moon by sighting along a stick pointed to one edge of the moon, and then sighting along a second stick pointed to the other edge. The angle that you measure between the two sticks is the angular diameter of the moon, and you would find that it is about a half degree.

So if you see a sphere that just covers the full moon, you know only that its angular diameter is one-half degree. But how big does it appear to be? That depends entirely on your impression of its distance. If you think this object is one hundred feet away, you will see it as about the size of a basketball; if you get the idea that it is a mile distant, you see it as being the size of a house. If it is moving sideways, you will see it traveling slowly if you think it is near, but rapidly if you perceive it to be far away.

So suppose a fellow were driving down the road, two hundred feet from where I have launched my three-foot-diameter balloon. It is late at night, and he is listening to music on the radio and trying to keep awake, when all of a sudden, off to his left, he sees this glowing orange sphere in the sky. If he makes the unconscious judgment that this unidentified object is a mile away, then what he "sees" is determined.

What he sees is an object eighty feet across, *the size of a spacecraft*. It rises straight up until it abruptly changes direction and, with an acceleration unmatched by any of our aircraft, takes off at three hundred miles per hour. Most amazing of all, after traveling at this high speed for ten seconds or so, it emits a brilliant flash—and disappears! He wouldn't have believed it if he hadn't seen it with his very own eyes.

I watched the newspaper for a notice of a new UFO sighting, but none was reported. My imagination takes me to a conversation with a "believer" who has read the detailed report of such a "reliable" observer, complete with numerical estimates of sizes and speeds. I might suggest that there are many possible explanations for such a sighting other than a secret government project or an alien spacecraft. Such as? Well, such as a searchlight on a cloud layer . . . or a superior mirage effect from a car on another road . . . or a college kid launching a paper balloon . . . or . . . . Come on, be reasonable . . . those are the suggestions of a closed-minded skeptic, grasping at straws.

Was I involved in science in launching that balloon? No, I was just playing.

Many examples of that kind of playing are associated in my mind with my long-time friend, Ray Newell, and the cabin we built, back in the woods, north of Lake Huron. That cabin is so important to me that I would like to tell you something of its history.

Ray and I roomed together in college, and after that we shared many activities: canoe trips, mountain climbing, bird watching, hiking, boomerang building and throwing, and many more. After we were married, he to Ellie, I to Barbara, I consider it to be one of the fortunate events of my life that our families became close friends, with connections between each of the individuals, connections that have persisted to this day. As our kids, and the Newells' Beth and Judy, were growing up, each summer we would meet and camp together somewhere between our homes in Milwaukee, Wisconsin, and Rochester, New York.

In 1971 we bought eighty acres of Canadian bush land, about halfway between our homes, and for a few years camped there together. Then we decided to build, with hand tools, a simple, primitive cabin in the woods, a quarter mile from the nearest gravel road. This involved transporting all the materials in to the building site on a two-wheeled cart that we built for that purpose. As we did it, we kept saying that we only had to do this once, and we would enjoy the isolation once the cabin was built. Even now, when I get to the cabin, having left the car on the gravel road and carried a few things in with me, I have something of the feeling of a child climbing up into a tree house and pulling the ladder up after me. So . . . now . . . here I am.

I sometimes have trouble explaining to people what there is to do in a place like that, but aside from the pleasures of having time and quiet surroundings in which to read, there is never a shortage of things to do. Ray is a knowledgeable amateur astronomer and comes with information about novas, or comets, or new satellite launches and their orbits, and the dark skies give good opportunity to see many of the things that are hidden by city lights near our homes. One year we saw that there must be some problem with the Russian spacecraft, *Progress*, that was to rendezvous with the orbiting space station, *Mir,* because we could see them separated as they passed over our cabin after they were scheduled to link up. Later reports confirmed that there were some docking problems that delayed the linkup. We, in our isolation, already had first-hand news of it.

There is a story, dating, I believe, back to the ancient Greeks, that stars can be seen during the day from the bottom of a deep-enough well. The basis for the story is probably not the sighting of stars but of Venus in the daylight sky. I have heard that Venus is visible in the daytime, even without the well, if you know where to look. Ray figured out where to look, and in the early afternoon of a clear day, we looked. We found it by searching the appropriate area of sky with binoculars and then found that we could remove the binoculars and see it perfectly well with the naked eye. In fact, it was obvious with the naked eye. Why had we never seen it before?

When we looked away and then looked back, it was gone. When we moved so that it was located just above the tip of a spruce tree, then we could see it, look elsewhere, and, knowing just where to look, could see it easily again with the unaided eye. Now the story about seeing the stars (Venus?) from the bottom of the well made more sense. Anything that isolated a small region of the sky containing Venus would make it easy to see. The explanation probably doesn't have anything to do with the darkness inside the well.

When we went to the woods to build the cabin, we had already picked out the site and had drawn up a design for the construction. In this part of the world the Canadian Shield, that great rocky formation that underlies much of northern and central Canada, is evident to the casual observer. Everywhere there are rocky outcroppings rounded by the action of the last glacier some ten thousand years ago. In our woods there are house-sized outcroppings surfacing every few hundred feet. Moving about the woods in the summertime is a process of diving into the woods, moving about submerged in the greenery, and emerging to the summer sky on a rounded rocky island thrust above the leafy sea.

We were going to build the cabin under a couple of white pine trees on the edge of the largest rock, which we had named Rock Centrum, in the middle of the property. The pole-building design called for the digging of six holes for upright posts, to which the structure of the cabin would be attached. After working for only a few minutes on the holes, something became very obvious that had not been obvious before. The layer of soil was very thin, and the excavation was more like a mining project than a digging project. On the spot we redesigned the cabin to be supported by surface rocks at the four corners. This involved translating the rectangle of the cabin to an adjacent site and rotating it until each corner was above a solid rock support, all at about the same height. Later we realized that we had inadvertently aligned the cabin rather close to the compass directions, with the long side along the north-south direction.

The alignment was close enough that the question arose whether we, in our meticulous planning for this structure, had chosen magnetic north for our reference, or had used true north, defined by the direction of the axis about which our earth rotates. Ray, my son Lee, and I answered the question one night by using a sighting compass to measure the deviation of our cabin line from true north, as determined by the direction of the North Star. We had maps telling us that magnetic north is five degrees west of true north. The result was that we had rather accurately bisected the angle between the two norths with our "careful" cabin alignment.

Before we went to sleep that night we thought about what the archeologists of the future might conclude when they examined the traces of this old cabin with its primitive construction techniques. What would they speculate about our culture when they realized that the alignment of the cabin so precisely split true north and what was, back in the late twentieth century, the direction of magnetic north in this region? It might be profound.

We did our own speculations about what we saw in the woods. We noticed on a warm summer day that in some shady places on the path the tops of rocks projecting above the ground were beaded with moisture. This observation set off a chain of events that has kept us amused for some time. The condensation on a rock indicates that the rock is cooler than the air—to be more specific, cooler than the dew point of the air. The soil is a better insulator than the rock, so the surface of the soil can warm up close to air temperature, even though the soil is cooler just below the surface. The rock is a better conductor of heat, and its surface temperature is closer to its temperature underground.

So this layer of moisture was telling us something about the underground temperature. We dug holes to measure the temperature at different depths below the surface and found that the temperature dropped in the first few inches and then remained rather constant over the next three feet or so, which was deep as we dug.

Would the temperature be low enough that we might use an underground pit as a cooler to keep milk and other perishables from spoiling?

We recorded the ground temperature measurements in the cabin log (the notebook where all such vital information is preserved) and wondered how the temperature in the hole behind the cabin would change over the year and, in fact, what temperature would make it useful for keeping food. The following year we had a men's get-together that included Ray, Lee, Jim Mallmann (who had worked with me on the simulation of ice-crystal halos), and me. Lee, living in North Carolina at the time, brought along the side of a milk carton from his local dairy, which gave the number of days for milk to sour at different temperatures. Here is the milk-carton data:

Temperature (Fahrenheit)	30	40	50	60	70	80
Days	24	10	2 to 5	1	1/2	1/2

Someone plotted the curve of "storage life" versus temperature in the log, and to people who understand such things, it looked as if it might have the form of a decreasing exponential curve. If it were an exponential curve, the plot of the logarithm of the lifetime against the temperature would give a straight line. Quickly a pocket calculator appeared, logarithms were determined, and when a surprisingly straight line appeared on the page of the notebook, someone did a least-squares fit to get its equation to a far greater accuracy than could ever be justified by the numbers on the milk carton. Sometimes an activity along the road is identified by warning signs proclaiming "Caution—Men at Work." These pages in the cabin log could proclaim "Caution—Boys at Play."

The cabin log is used to record: the comings and goings of people who have been there, the size of the spring morel harvest, information about birds and animals seen, the state of the beaver impoundment and its inhabitants, an annual report on the size of the various wild-orchid colonies, the quality of the latest wildberry cobbler-type desert baked in the rock oven, the abundance of the meteor shower, the splendor of the northern lights, observations on the morning-long activities of a spider spinning the web on the front porch, thoughts, and speculations. Ellie frequently records some of her impressions or thoughts in verse. Consider a sample of her work (with a perfunctory nod to Ogden Nash):

I look like an Amazon
When I have pajamas on.
But when I wear a nightie
I look like Aphrodite.

Each of us has his or her own style, and each is always eager to read what the log tells of happenings since we were last there.

Our daughter, Karen, with her background in theater, professes to see those pages of milk-keeping analysis in the cabin log as a comedy, not for a minute being taken in by the ridiculous premise that reasonable persons would do mathematics like that, when they didn't have to, under the pretense of playing. She might affect a similar attitude toward the calculation that allows the rain barrel, which collects runoff water from the roof, to be used as a rain gauge.

That kind of discussion, of course, goes both ways. When we fantasize that I might perform on the glass harmonica on the streets of Milwaukee during the "Alewives Festival," with Lee accompanying on the guitar, we agree that Karen can design the costumes and be in charge of the "cheap theatrics." It is lost on none of us, however, that among many of her groups of colleagues, Karen is the one who keeps up with science developments and serves the role in those groups as local expert in matters of physical and natural science.

Our measurements show that a pit in the ground would have a temperature of about forty-five degrees Fahrenheit in early June, at which temperature milk would keep for about six days without souring. That seemed promising. I obtained a large plastic container with a wide-mouth, screw-on lid that was originally used to ship olives in wholesale lots. When it was installed in the pit behind the cabin, it became the olive-pit cooler.

One of the cabin rituals is to measure the olive-pit temperature at each arrival and, of course, record the data in the log. A plot of this temperature over the year shows the temperature rising from about forty-five degrees at the beginning of June to a high of fifty-five in early August, and back to forty-five degrees in early October. The occasional data points in early January show twenty-eight degrees, the same as the low temperature recorded one winter by a max/min thermometer left in the pit. We were somewhat surprised by the consistency of the temperatures from year to year. When the temperatures from the last dozen years are all plotted together as a function of day and month, they lie, with some scatter, on the same curve.

We realized that, without intending to, we had constructed a calendar. By measuring the temperature in the olive pit and referring to our plotted curve, we can deduce the date. How accurately can we tell the date from this hole in the ground? To answer that question, we have to look at the smooth curve we draw through the data points and at the scatter of the points about the curve. It would be most accurate in April or October when the temperature is changing at the rate of a degree every two or three days and much less accurate in August, near the temperature maximum, when the temperature is changing very little from day to day. In the spring or fall, if we were to lose track of the date, it appears we could, with our marvelous calendar, measure the temperature in the olive pit and determine the date to an accuracy of about six days.

There are a number of things we could do to improve the accuracy of the system: we could use a digital thermometer to measure temperature more accurately than to the nearest degree; we could be sure to always make the measurement early in the morning to avoid the slight variation that takes place over the length of a sunny day; we could be sure that the board cover on the pit is always shaded from the sun; we could make that cover fit tighter to keep outside air from leaking in; and we could even bury the thermometer in a small, deeper cavity made just for the purpose, rather than compromising the temperature measurement by storing food in the pit. Actually, if we did improve the accuracy of the measurements, we might be able to relate the variations from year to year to the local variation in the yearly average temperature.

As we thought about it, we realized that the deeper in the ground we go, the smaller the variation between summer and winter temperatures would be. In our pit in the summer the temperature is below the air temperature, probably averaging the air temperature over a time period of two or three months. At some greater depth the averaging time would be several months, with the result that the temperature variation over a year would be further reduced. And, deeper yet, we would find the earth temperature constant over the year, as if the earth were averaging the air temperature over a period of a few years. At that depth the only temperature changes we would expect to see would be slower changes—slow drift in the average earth temperature that results from changes in the average temperature of the air at the earth's surface. There is a lot of interest in global warming. Is this a cheap and easy way to monitor it? Maybe.

Another idea developed as we talked about our olive-pit temperatures. It takes time for a temperature change in the air to penetrate into the earth. If we were to measure the temperature of the earth at some depth, for example, where the temperature is effectively a ten-year average, it would be the ten-year average, not of the air temperature over the last decade, but of a decade of perhaps twenty years ago. That idea suggests that the history of the surface air temperature of our planet is preserved underground, waiting for us to decipher it. A colleague pointed out that this is not an original idea; an article in *Science* explores the possibility of measuring temperatures in deep, oil-well bore holes to see if they give any evidence for global temperature change. Still, the idea might yield some interesting results.

Are we going to do all of those things to improve the temperature measurements in our olive pit? I don't know—probably not. After all, we are only playing.

One summer at the cabin we played at blowing bubbles with a newly marketed device consisting of a loop of webbing material that can be dipped into a detergent solution and then spread to make a source of giant bubbles. With practice we could launch bubbles three feet in diameter or, in a slight wind, could make cylindrical bubbles ten or twelve feet long. The long bubbles are not stable but rather quickly break up into smaller bubbles. They do last long enough to be captured on film, however, and I have a number of very nice photos of those great bubbles. I have used those pictures of soap bubbles to show the beautiful interference colors evident in light reflected off a thin soap film, and I have used the pictures to teach students or public audiences about the interference of light waves.

But as I looked at those bubble photos sometime later, I had the feeling there was something there that I didn't understand, although I hadn't consciously questioned it. I am familiar with this process in other circumstances; it is as if I am trying to avoid asking a question to which I may not know the answer.

The photos were taken on Rock Centrum, surrounded by trees. When looking at the photos one more time, I noticed that in the bubble you can see an image of a horizontal band of dark trees, with a lighter background both above and below. It seems natural to associate that band of trees with the trees in the background of the photo. But when I thought of it, I realized that it was not obvious what kind of focusing action could cause that kind of an image. Once the question was posed, I could think about the explanation. It seemed to me that the optics of a bubble are simple enough that if I couldn't explain the image that was so obvious in those photos, then someone would be justified in revoking my license to practice optics.

The answer to the question was suggested to me by a bubble photo I had taken a few years earlier. It is a self-portrait, taken of my reflection in a soap bubble. The surprising thing is that there is not one reflected image, but two—and one of them is upside down. The explanation of the two images is simple. The front side of the bubble reflects some of the light, and this curved soap film acts like a convex mirror, producing a reflected image of my face, reduced in size and in a "normal" upright orientation. The back surface of the bubble acts as a concave mirror and produces an inverted image of my face that I can also see—and photograph. When we understand the two images seen in this "portrait" photo, we can understand the band of trees seen in the giant bubble floating over Rock Centrum. The band of trees in the bubble is not an image of the trees beyond the bubble but a reflected image of the trees behind my back. In fact, there are two images, one upright and one inverted, and their superposition gives the bright image of the sky both above and below the band of trees.

A few years later I wrote an article titled "Looking Into a Bubble" for *Optics and Photonics News*, a monthly news magazine for the optical science and engineering community. I showed the giant bubble photos as a puzzle for the reader to explain. The self portrait was shown in the back of the magazine as a clue to the explanation, and a discussion of the explanation was given. It was not a profound article, but apparently some readers did enjoy it. (It was not intended to be profound—we were really just playing, next to the cabin, on Rock Centrum.)

To aid in the discussion of the two images I included diagrams that showed the reflected light from the front and back surfaces of the bubble. The rays reflected off the concave back surface are focused to form a real image, in the same way that a telescope mirror forms a real image of a planet. In optics the description of an image as "real" has a technical meaning. It means that the light rays actually converge to form an image in space (in this case, inside the bubble). The image exists and can be displayed on a piece of paper held right there. This is in contrast to the image formed by the light reflected from the front surface of the bubble.

After reflection the light rays from the front surface diverge, never actually converging to a focus. The light rays diverge *as if they were coming from a focus inside the bubble,* and we can see an image there, but it is not a real image; it is called a virtual image. You have daily experiences with virtual images; for example, you are looking at a virtual image of yourself when you brush your teeth in the morning. Your image appears to be located behind the mirror surface, but there is really nothing there; no image will appear on a piece of paper moved around behind the mirror. It is a virtual image that you are viewing.

Discussing the nature of those two images gave me the inspiration (and the excuse) to end the bubble article with an illustration of how scientific terminology is determined, clearly, one might assume, an important matter in the development of science. In the case of the two reflected images from the bubble, we see that the orientation of the real image is inverted and that of the virtual image is upright. This is generally true whether the images are formed by a mirror or by a lens, and that idea led to an incident that began in the 1970s and ended only recently.

When Peter Franken of the University of Arizona in Tucson was president of the Optical Society of America in the 1970s, he announced a limerick contest. The limerick had to relate to optics, and there were prizes for the winners. As I recall, Peter offered as first prize a thirty-centimeter-tall cactus, and as second prize two thirty-centimeter-tall cacti! With an election year coming up, I had an idea for a limerick that

I worked out shortly after seeing the contest announcement. The limerick played on the different meanings of the words "upright" and "real" when they are applied to optical images and when they are applied to public images constructed by aspiring politicians. I suspected that if I submitted my entry six months before the deadline, it would get lost, since entries are almost never received until a week before (or after) the deadline. So I waited. Here was my entry.

> *To a politician who would reveal*
> *An image with public appeal,*
> *Said his optical friend,*
> *"In my view I contend*
> *If it's Upright it's Virtual, Not Real!"*

Unfortunately, when I remembered the tucked-away limerick more than six months later, I had missed the deadline, and someone else had won the fame and the cactus.

A dozen years later I was sitting at a scientific meeting next to Robert Resnick, author and coauthor of a series of textbooks that have helped educate generations of students in physics. Knowing that he is a connoisseur of limericks, I recalled the contest and my failed entry and wrote it on a napkin to show him. He laughed and put the napkin in his pocket, and I promptly forgot the incident.

When I ran into him a couple of months later, he greeted me with some enthusiasm, saying, "Good news! We're going to use your limerick."

"What?"

"I showed your poem to Halliday, and he liked it so much that we are including it in our new edition."

"My poem?"

I slowly recalled our dinner-table conversation as he explained more carefully to me that he had shown the limerick napkin to his coauthor, David Halliday. The third edition of their *Fundamentals of Physics* was in the galley-proof stage. Halliday, who was responsible for the optics section, had referred in the book to the virtual images, formed by lenses or mirrors, as being "erect" images. However, he liked the poem well enough that he went through the proofs and, whenever there was a reference to an "erect" image, he changed it to "upright" image, so that he could include the poem in the third edition. So if you thought that all decisions about scientific terminology are made by a room full of serious people gathered about a large conference table in Geneva or Paris, now you know how it really happens.

I have given some examples of how mathematics became involved in our playing with the milk-carton data at the cabin. I think of other examples of my playing where some simple mathematics significantly influenced my perception of what I had observed. That is, I "saw" something different with the use of mathematics than I would have seen without it. My laboratory at Allis Chalmers was a well-lit, air-conditioned room. The window next to my desk looked out on the landscape of an old industrial plant, with its rusty storage bins, grimy buildings, and dirt-filled corners. On one of the first sunny, cool days of an autumn season a movement just outside the window caught my attention, and I glanced up just in time to see a monarch butterfly flit past. After it happened again, I went to look out the window and saw another and another go by.

These beautiful butterflies seemed out of place in this industrial environment, but as I watched I saw that there was a steady procession moving south along this building. Their flight corridor seemed to extend only about fifty feet out from the leeward side of my block-long, five-story building. I talked by phone to a person whose window was eighty feet from mine and started a timer when he reported a passing butterfly. As the orange and black creature came dancing past my window, I stopped the timer and computed the flying speed. They were traveling about seven miles per hour. I measured the flux of butterflies flowing past, outside my window. Each hour I did a three-minute count and recorded the number of butterflies that passed my window in that three-minute interval. The numbers increased as the morning proceeded, then dropped off again in the afternoon. I recorded numbers like 30, 60, 12, 9 butterflies in my three-minute samples—butterflies moving faster than a person could walk, along my building to the south.

The monarchs were moving, and I was excited to realize that this stretch of wind-protected flight I was watching was only one city block of a flight that would continue for over a thousand miles, a flight that would carry these fragile, helpless bits of color from Canada to Mexico. It was a journey almost unimaginable for something with the perceived frivolous nature of a butterfly but which, nevertheless, would be accomplished despite gusty winds, cold driving rains, and a scorching hot sun. If I could believe that such an impossible trip could be made, then I could also accept that these same individuals would start the trip back north in the spring and that in the summer I would see their descendants come to lay their eggs on the milkweed plants in the fields around my house.

What did my three-minute counts, 30, 60, 12, 9, mean? I could see that around noon there was a peak flow of twenty butterflies each minute traveling down this narrow flyway. The number dropped over the next four hours to one per minute, then to none. But what is one butterfly per minute, or even twenty? Had I seen a few butterflies? or several? or even many? Here some simple mathematics shaped my perception. When I plotted the butterfly counts against the time of day, a smooth curve resulted. The area under that curve yielded the total number of butterflies whose passage I had sampled. I could see that what I had witnessed on this day was three thousand butterflies pulsing past my dingy window, where I watched them fly a few yards of their thousand-mile journey—where I watched them and marveled.

Another example comes to mind of the pleasure of using mathematics in solving a mundane problem. We moved into an old farmhouse outside Milwaukee, and we did some remodeling to make it comfortable for our lifestyle. Into the large farm kitchen we put a window ten feet wide that gives us a view to the rear of the house, including some mowed area, prairie plantings, an orchard, brushy patches, trees, fields, bird feeders, and the hundreds of wild things that inhabit, or drift through, such an environment. With a large table in front of the window, this becomes the place where we eat all of our meals, the scene before us equally interesting in spring, summer, fall, and winter. We needed a table to fit the size and shape of the space in front of the window. What would fit well was something with a sort of elliptical shape, about eight feet long and four feet wide. I decided to design it and have it made by a kitchen-cabinetmaker.

To draw the ellipse on the four-by-eight-foot sheet of plywood, I drove two nails into the surface and surrounded them by a loop of string. A pencil moved around the inside of this loop traces out an ellipse. But when I had adjusted the spacing between the nails and the length of the string loop to give me a four-by-eight-foot ellipse, I was not satisfied by the shape; it was too pointy on the ends. Another geometric figure that would have answered this objection is a semicircle on each end of a rectangle, but that was not a pleasing shape.

So what shape could it be? What if, instead of running the loose loop of string around two nails, I ran it around four nails, located at the corners of a rectangle. If the width of the rectangle were made very narrow, the figure drawn by the pencil in the loop would approach the ellipse. If the width were increased, and the loop were made nearly tight around the four nails, the figure would approach a rectangle with slightly bulgy sides and rounded corners. And somewhere, between these extremes, was an aesthetically pleasing form, similar to an ellipse but with the ends just a bit blunter. I wanted a name for this form; what should I call it?

Think of starting to draw this (unnamed) shape with the pencil in the loop of string tracing out the long side of the figure. The ends of the loop of string, which determine the pencil position, are defined by the two nails on that long side of the rectangle. In fact, what is being traced out is exactly the ellipse dictated by those two nails, as if the others were not there. But when the pencil moves beyond the end of the rectangle, it reaches a point where the string leaves that corner nail, and the loop is constrained by the two nails on opposite corners of the rectangle. It is now tracing an ellipse dictated by these two nails on the opposite corners, a second ellipse that connects smoothly to the first. As the pencil is moved further around the end of the figure, the loop of string becomes constrained by the two nails on the end of the rectangle, tracing out yet a third ellipse that connects, without the slightest discontinuity, to the second.

The figure that results from moving the pencil in the loop of string all the way around the four nails is composed of pieces of eight different ellipses, connected seamlessly into a graceful figure that was to be the shape of our kitchen table. Since I had discovered it, I had the privilege of naming it. I called it an octellipse.

Was I really the first person to discover this geometric shape? Probably not. I never tried to search the mathematical literature to see if it had been mentioned before and never tried to tell the world about it. Although we like the table, it is no big deal. Most people refer to it as an oval, but I take pleasure in knowing that it is an octellipse, and I know that on the day that I figured it out, I won the game that I was playing.

We have some other furniture that has an original design. I had thought for a few years about building some wooden benches. It would be nice to be able to sit in the woods to see what is moving through the trees on a summer morning, to sit back at the corner of the woods and watch the geese come into the cornfield in the fall, and to sit along the big road-side prairie when twenty or thirty species of native flowering plants are all in bloom at the same time. In fact, I could use several benches. And my children all live in places where they would gladly use one or more benches. But my impression is that most wooden benches are really not designed to be comfortable. If I were going to make several of them, it might be worth some effort to find a good design.

Whenever I passed a park bench or a bench in front of a store in a small town, I would sit in it, thinking that I would find a good design that I could copy. There are many benches that, despite looking attractive, are really uncomfortable. For example, the back of the bench may be of such a shape that, although it consists of three boards, the back of a seated person only touches the top one. It would look strange to omit the other two boards, but it wouldn't make any difference to the comfort of someone sitting on the bench. I have seen plans for a simple, attractive bench designed by Aldo Leopold, the Wisconsonite whose *Sand County Almanac* has shaped the ecological movement in our country. I thought that I might copy his design, until I sat on one of the benches. Though he may have shaped an environmental movement, he did not shape a wooden bench that fits my body. It seemed to me that the problem required an experimental approach.

An old horse stall in the barn became the site for the bench-development project. I nailed a horizontal two-by-four on each wall of the stall, fifteen inches above the floor. These supported the ends of the three two-by-fours that were to constitute the seat. By putting blocks and wedges under the ends of the seat boards, I could experiment with the height, spacing, and shape of the seat. A back was provided by nailing support legs on a wooden pallet so that it stood up, sloped backward slightly more than was appropriate. The slope could be adjusted by putting various numbers of blocks under the back of the support legs. Some leftover lengths of wooden siding served as wedge-shaped boards that, when clamped to the pallet, gave a curvature to the back that could be adjusted till it approximated the curvature of a human spine.

Two important variables were left to be determined: the slope of the back and the distance of the back from the seat. This was the state of the project at Thanksgiving time, when there was a gathering of the family for a holiday celebration. After dinner a group of people went with me out to the barn to be a part of the bench-design exercise. I gave them what I called the optometrist test. "Sit right down here and make yourself comfortable," I would say. "Now, which arrangement do you find more comfortable, A or" (I would move the back one centimeter away from the seat) "B? You say B? Okay, do you prefer B or" (I would put another block under the support legs) "C? Now C? . . . or D? How about C? . . . or E?"

Each comparison was with a different combination of back angle and distance from the seat. I was surprised at how consistent each person was in his or her selection of optimum positions, as I came back to them through the series of choices. After a few minutes in the seat, each person yielded numbers for the two variables. Averaging the numbers for the nine Greenlers who took the test gave me the design, a design that should be a good compromise, at least for those nine people. I had the name for the bench that resulted from this procedure: The Greenler Consensus Bench.

Actually, what I had determined was the position in space of the six surfaces—three in the seat and two in the back—that defined the contact between wood and body. How those surfaces become fixed in space is, of course, a significant part of the design. By borrowing some ideas from the Aldo Leopold bench, I came up with something that pleases me with the efficiency of its parts.

Was it really necessary to get that many people involved to figure out how to design a simple outdoor bench? Of course not. But people do things much stranger than that in their playing.

The Consensus Bench

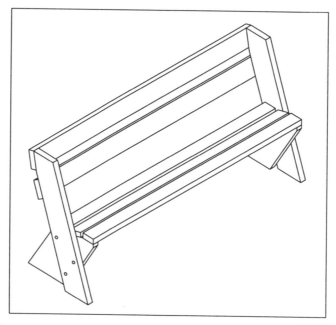

Materials:
-Approximately 7 ft. of 2x8 for long legs
-Approximately 4 ft. of 2x12 for short legs
-2 lengths of 2x6 as long as the bench
-3 lengths of 2x4 three inches shorter than the bench
    (40 inches is a reasonable length for two people and 56
    inches is about right for three.)
-6 carriage bolts 3/8" by 3 1/2" long with nuts and washers
-Screws for assembly (drill driven deck screws work well)

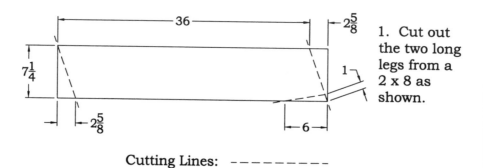

1. Cut out the two long legs from a 2 x 8 as shown.

Cutting Lines: - - - - - - - -

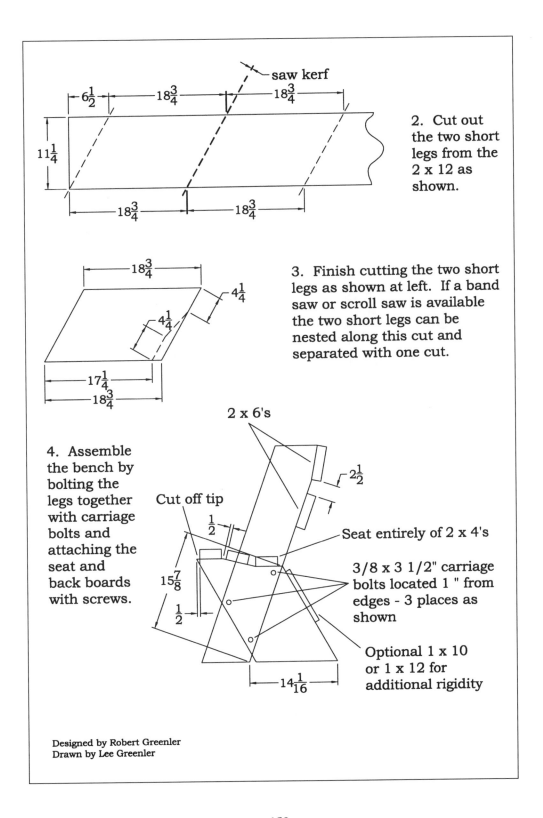

2. Cut out the two short legs from the 2 x 12 as shown.

3. Finish cutting the two short legs as shown at left. If a band saw or scroll saw is available the two short legs can be nested along this cut and separated with one cut.

4. Assemble the bench by bolting the legs together with carriage bolts and attaching the seat and back boards with screws.

2 x 6's

Cut off tip

Seat entirely of 2 x 4's

3/8 x 3 1/2" carriage bolts located 1 " from edges - 3 places as shown

Optional 1 x 10 or 1 x 12 for additional rigidity

Designed by Robert Greenler
Drawn by Lee Greenler

The Consensus Bench

In our society there is a cultural attitude that permits and encourages young boys and girls to play with toys. When the boys grow into men, playing with toys is not considered appropriate, unless the toys are expensive, like pickup trucks or power boats. It is less obvious to me what the toy-substitute for women is. I have told a class of students, as I demonstrated some principle of physics in the operation of a mechanical toy, that if they play their cards right, they might not have to give up toys when they grow up.

But this is a cultural attitude that is not the same everywhere. We lived in Malaysia, where I taught for a year. There, kite flying and top spinning have a long cultural tradition, and it is interesting to see that it is carried on by adult men. Some of the best contacts I had that year with people away from the University and the city where we were living were through kites and tops. The metaphor that comes to mind is that sharing an interest in tops would let me stand beside another person looking at the spinning top and talking about life, which is much easier than standing facing another person wishing there were some way we could talk about our very different lives.

When my son, Lee, and his wife, Susan, came to visit us in Malaysia, we arranged to visit a kite flyer I had met, who lived outside a small town some distance from Kuala Lumpur. He took us to visit his friend, the local top maker, and when Lee presented the top maker with a beautiful top that he (Lee) had made on his lathe at home, our welcome was assured. We were accepted into the brotherhood, and the top maker showed us the secret of how he balances his tops, the secret that enabled the local group to win competitions with groups from all over the country. He trusted that we would not reveal the secret to other Malaysian top makers.

The word was passed that in the afternoon there would be a kite fly and, in an open place at the edge of the village, people kept appearing until there were fifteen or twenty kites in the sky. People sat on the ground in small groups, watching the kites and visiting. The kites were handled by the men, but the women were also there, and the kids running around acted like kids everywhere. Their initial shyness toward us was overcome by the excitement of Barbara's offer to let each child pick one "lucky stone" from her collection of small polished stones. I don't know how we could have arranged, or have been invited to, such a relaxed, friendly gathering if we had set out directly to do it.

Before we left Malaysia, I visited the town of Kota Baru, in the northeast corner of the country, where there is a tradition of top spinning distinct from that of the rest of the country. In most of Malaysia the traditional top is four or five inches in diameter and weighs between one and two pounds. In Kota Baru they make a top out of a combination of wood and tin that is about eight inches in diameter and weighs seven pounds. Tin, which is plentiful in Malaysia, is used as a heavy metal for things like fishing sinkers and weighted tops, in applications where we would use lead. The heavy tops are difficult to throw, and even the top spinners in the rest of

Malaysia don't know how to throw the Kota Baru top.

The process is one of several steps, each requiring considerable skill. First, the latex-treated rope has to be wound very tightly around the top so that when the top is thrown, it is forced to unwind from the rope, which sets it spinning. If the rope slips, the top does not spin. The thrower assumes the throwing position and pauses, trying to keep in his mind all of the elements of the motion that are necessary for a successful launch. A convulsive motion sends the top flying toward a raised mound of clay about three feet on a side. When the top lands, it is quickly scooped up on a wooden paddle by a waiting participant. When he has it spinning stably on the paddle, he pulls from his belt a turned cylinder of wood with a concave disc of metal set in the end and carefully maneuvers the top from the paddle onto the metal disc. He passes it to the next participant, who meditates on its motion until, satisfied that it is spinning appropriately, sets it into a section of bamboo, partially buried in the ground, where it will continue to spin and spin and spin. The local legend is that the top will spin for about an hour, unless a spirit should enter the top and keep it spinning for twenty-four hours. I saw one top that had been spinning for slightly more than an hour when the owner stopped it so that he could go home.

I brought back a Kota Baru top for me, one for Lee, and one for my son-in-law, John, who is also a maker and spinner of tops. We three have played with tops and talked about things that we might do together with tops. I decided I could present a *Science Bag* program on tops, which would give me an excuse to spend some time on things that I would like to do anyway. The result was a presentation, "Why Does a Spinning Top Stop?"

This program, which is preserved in a videotape version, presented something of the history of tops and gave a description of various classes of tops. Of course, I demonstrated the action of many different tops. The heart of the program was an attempt to explain to a public audience the mechanics of rotating bodies. When at the end we were able to answer the question posed in the title, we had all of the pieces to see what we might do to make a top spin as long as possible.

My attempt to apply these insights to a freely spinning peg top (not a gyroscope top supported by bearings) resulted in a top made of a truck tire filled with water so that the whole thing weighed 220 pounds. It has a steel axle, rounded at the end, and, like the Kota Baru top, spins on a (hardened) concave steel surface. I had not really finished the development of the tire top when the time came for the first *Science Bag* performance, but I showed the audience what it could do and what improvements I was working on. By the end of the month I could start the top at the beginning of the program by spinning it up to speed with a heavy-duty electric drill and have it still spinning an hour later when the presentation came to a close.

We might try some more improvements to make this giant tire top spin longer, but I probably won't pursue them. I was impressed that my efforts didn't yield a longer spinning top than those hand-thrown Kota Baru tops, even those spinning without the presence of a spirit.

The answer to the question, "Why does a spinning top stop?" is that it stops because of torques that oppose its motion. There are two obvious torques, both resulting from a kind of friction. One is from friction between the spinning tip and the surface on which it is spinning, and the other is from air drag. The question is not a very subtle one, and it would not take most physicists long to come up with that answer.

But I can say, "Look at this little peg top, which I can spin like this (between my thumb and middle finger), and it spins nicely like that . . . changing its motion as it slows down . . . and, in fifteen seconds, falls over. Which of those torques, tip friction or air drag, is the dominant one? Or what about the traditional Malaysian top that can spin for five minutes? Which force is the more important in slowing it down?" Then the answers are not so obvious. I am willing to bet that most physicists would not have any good intuition about the relative sizes of the two friction effects.

If you like to play with such things, you might think about finding out. For a given type of spinning motion—when the top is "sleeping," for instance, spinning with no wandering or tilting of its axis—the friction effect on the tip is constant and should not be getting larger or smaller as the top slows down. On the other hand, the effect of air drag should change significantly with the rotation speed of the top. The effect of air drag should build up very rapidly as the top is spun faster and should go to zero as the speed of rotation goes to zero.

So for any top, air drag should dominate if it is spinning fast enough, and tip friction should dominate when it is spinning slow enough. Perhaps, then, a nice way to answer the question about which effect is the dominant one for different tops is to determine when, in its spinning time, the top makes the transition between these two regimes.

Another way to ask the same question is: When, after the top is spun, are the two friction effects exactly the same size? If the time when these forces are just the same is just before the top falls over, then it would be reasonable to say that such a top is dominated by air drag. On the other hand, if the time comes just after you have launched the top, that top is dominated by tip friction. The extreme case of a top dominated by tip friction is one which you can not spin fast enough to reach that equal-friction point.

If some persons were interested enough to measure the speed of rotation of a top from the time it is launched until it falls over, and if they did some mathematics to predict how this speed should change under the two kinds of friction torques, then by comparing the theory with the data, they ought to be able to answer the question. "But who," you might ask, "would be willing to go to all that effort to answer such a question when there is no real need to know the answer?"

"Well, who," I might ask in reply, "would spend days and years of his or her life in trying to find out how few whacks of the stick it can take to knock a little white ball into the hole clear at the other end of the long lawn? Or how little time to run around the big circle four times?" Many of us are willing to invest significant effort in our playing.

One time John, Lee, and I got together in my lab to spin a variety of tops and videotape their performance. We added a radial line to the upper surface of each top. By looking at the position of that line on two successive video frames, we should be able to measure the rotation speed of the top. We should also be able to analyze the curve of rotation speed as a function of time to get our answer. But we also came up with another method of separating the two effects. We recorded the spinning of the tops when we spun them inside a chamber that could be quickly evacuated by a vacuum pump. In a short time we removed the air drag by removing the air. We haven't gotten around to analyzing the data on that videotape yet, but

I expect that we will and will probably publish the results in an appropriate place.

Although John is my son-in-law, his last name is Greenler. You might speculate on the various motivations we have for this project and wonder whether any part is played by the prospect of publishing a paper authored by Greenler, Greenler, and Greenler. Well, why not? After all, we're only playing.

> **So how do I respond to this guy in the back row who is suggesting that all of this stuff I have been telling them about the origins of these sky effects is really nothing more than my amusing myself with my little games?**

A familiar experience for me is that it is three o'clock the next morning when I finally come up with the answer that I should have given to such a confrontational question—and by four o'clock I have an even better answer. But this night was different; the answer I gave, on the spot, is essentially the answer I would have given at four o'clock in the morning, or even a few years later.

> **"I really don't think of an answer to your question—but I think of a few different answers. In the first place, it seems to me to be something of a strange question. If I were performing a Beethoven sonata, and the audience were as involved and appreciative as I perceive this one is tonight, you would not have asked the question; you would have assumed that the pleasure of the audience justified the long hours of study and practice that I had invested in preparing myself for the performance. It is a little strange that, once you label my performance 'science,' you require more than the aesthetic experience to justify it.**

> **"A second response that comes to mind is that the beginnings of our science lay in people's attempts to explain the things that they saw in the world around them. Certainly what I have described tonight is directly in that tradition. If you think that science has been successful, in that the system has come up with good ways to answer some of the questions we ask, then I would think you**

would hesitate to tinker with the ground rules under which it has prospered.

"And I think of a third answer. I guess I must admit that to a large degree, you are right. My motivation for looking into these beautiful effects was just to enjoy them; to a large extent I was just playing. The computer simulations were an attempt to understand what kind of ice crystals could produce these fascinating displays in the sky, and my photos were an attempt to collect them. When I started out, I did not anticipate that later more than one meteorologist would tell me that my book had been useful to them in using the optical sky effects as remote indicators of the kind of ice crystals that are in the atmosphere— something very important for meteorologists investigating the large-scale air circulation over the earth. And it's surprising how often that sort of thing happens."

The audience claps and cheers; I think they understand.

Chapter Thirteen

CHOICES

Today's mail brings an invitation. The "Discussion
Group" is invited to gather at a friend's home for an
evening.

Forty years ago we were meeting every couple of months to discuss
some political, social, or ethical problem. There was no organization.
Someone would mail out an article as introductory reading and give the
subject, date, and place for the next gathering. If no one took the initiative,
there was no gathering. This was not a subgroup of some organization but
an accretion of people who enjoyed the wide-open discussions and
became friends based on this contact. Most such informal groups seem to
have a finite lifetime, and, after a few years, the called evenings for this
group became less regular and then ceased—ceased, that is, except for
the party around Christmas time, when we exchanged white-elephant
gifts, played charades, and kept in touch with each others' lives. And
then, after many years, we seemed to get so busy with other things that
the annual party also ceased.

> So here is a call for the group to gather again. The invita-
> tion mentions those days of "discussions when we were
> young and thought there were answers to all the problems
> of the world" and goes on to ask, "So what have we
> learned in all these years of living? We should know more
> now than we did then." It ends with the assignment "to

write out something that you have learned and put into practice. Make copies for everyone and bring them along." Well, that's a real challenge.

It seems that much of what I have learned is intimately tied up with the choices I have made; the choices flow from what I have learned, and what I learn is shaped by the consequences of choices I have made. This is true both for my professional life and for other parts of my life, these various parts that press against each at many different boundaries and often overlap.

I think of a phone call I received while I was working in Berlin. Here was a call that challenged me to make some new choices, to shift some of the boundaries between my professional and private life. It was from the Program Director at the National Science Foundation, who supervised the research grant that supported my surface-science work. Before I can tell you of the significance of the call to me, I must explain how the research-grant system works.

I had been fortunate to continue to get modest NSF support for my surface work for the previous twenty years. Although the grants were not large, in general they supported a couple of graduate students and provided funds to help keep the laboratory equipment operating. This support was supplemented by occasional grants from a trust fund set up to support basic research, the Petroleum Research Fund administered by the American Chemical Society, and some money available through the Laboratory for Surface Studies. The NSF grants were usually for a period of three years.

NSF supports a variety of activities, and different programs have different procedures for evaluating proposals. The process for funding the kind of research I do with students in my laboratory begins with a research proposal that finds its way to a Program Director who is responsible for providing funding in a particular scientific area. The Director seeks the advice of three to six experts in the field of the proposal to help evaluate its scientific merit and the probability that the proposer will be able to do what he or she proposes to do. This latter judgment has to do with the past record of accomplishment of the researcher.

The Program Director is required to seek the written evaluation of working scientists for these proposals, but he or she is responsible for making the final judgment, within the NSF guidelines. On request, after a decision has been made on a grant proposal, NSF will send the proposer a copy of the comments and overall evaluation of each reviewer, in a form that maintains the anonymity of the reviewers. The overall evaluation is indicated by checking a box for the categories: *excellent, very good, good,* or *unacceptable.*

Periodically this peer-review system comes up for criticism in Congress or the press, and charges of bias or corruption in the system are leveled. Surely the possibility for bias is inherent in a system where the people with a significant input into funding decisions are those actively involved in the same field, working and competing with one another and all trying to get support from a limited number of inadequate sources. The alternatives are to have such decisions made by people who don't understand the content of the proposals, or to have the award be a political process.

And sometimes vocal Congressional critics of the system are those who wangle support for a program in a university or hospital in their district by appending the budget item to a totally unrelated piece of legislation, and getting it passed by a process that is totally unrelated to the merit of the program. What comes to mind is a comment of Winston Churchill on democracy, which I might paraphrase: "The peer-review system is the worst possible way to award research support—with the exception of all others." Actually, my view of the system is more positive than that; I think it generally works quite well.

The record of a scientist's research, published in research journals, provides one of the more objective measures of his or her accomplishments. The reputable journals all use peer review to help decide what papers to accept for publication and to suggest or require changes where scientific standards are not met. Those who want to dramatize the publish-or-perish effect in academic survival sometimes claim that the only thing that matters is the number of publications, their quality or significance being irrelevant. Most exaggerations start with some kernel of truth, and there is some significance attached to the number of publications.

But the closer one is to the field of the researcher, the less important becomes the number. Papers in journals with more rigorous review policies count for more than papers published in fringe journals with less rigorous standards. A paper that is one of a series of short papers making the same type of measurement on a series of different materials may have less significance than a paper describing a new method for investigating an effect. And if you are familiar with the literature of a scientific field, you can judge the contribution made by a person far more effectively than someone can by *counting* his published papers.

Over the years in which I received modest-sized research grants from NSF, I typically published a couple papers a year on my surface research. I would sometimes see a reviewer's comment to the effect that Greenler's work is careful and of high quality, but there is not a lot of it. Such comments would frequently be followed by a high evaluation. It is my impression, which may or may not be true, that such evaluations are made relatively independent of the size of the grant support. Another related impression, either true or untrue, is that NSF expectations for productivity are not proportional to the level of grant support; one can't successfully propose to get grant support that is half of a "typical" award and keep it by producing half of the "typical" results.

The phone call in Berlin from the NSF Program Director concerned a proposal for a three-year grant renewal that I had submitted before going to Berlin. He was speaking about renewal in pessimistic terms. He reported that although I had gotten reasonable ratings, some reviewers had questioned my productivity during the past three years. I acknowledged it and said that I had a number of things just recently completed that either had been submitted for publication or were now in preparation. He and I both understand that a manuscript "in preparation" counts for little—some manuscripts are "in preparation" for years. A manuscript "submitted for publication" gets points for activity but, given the reality of the reviewing system, doesn't count much for results. On the other hand, a manuscript "accepted for publication" by such-and-such a journal and available in preprint form counts nearly as much as the published work.

In such a situation he said he would usually do one of three things: fund a new three-year grant, give a one-year grant and then terminate NSF support, or cut off support with a small amount of money to help finish up the current semester's activity.

There followed several moments of silence, clearly transmitted over the long-distance telephone lines that linked West Berlin, Germany, to Washington, D.C., U.S.A. Finally, he said that because I had done good work in the past, and my work has the reputation for being careful and reliable, he was going to fund me for one more year to give me a chance to complete enough work to make a stronger grant application. And he ended the conversation by giving me some serious advice: if I were to expect to continue to get NSF support, I would have to concentrate my efforts on this work and not dilute them by playing around with other things.

I spent time the next few days walking the streets of Berlin, kicking pebbles off the sidewalk. Who had put this man in charge of my life?! What he was telling me was that if I wanted to continue doing surface science with NSF support, I should quit running *The Science Bag*, stop accepting invitations to talk to public groups about science, avoid getting involved in the appearance of butterfly wings, give up the idea of spending Saturdays in family activities, quit chasing rainbows. . . . His "advice" sounded like a threat that I could ignore only at my own peril. I had to respond with a decision about the priorities in my life.

I decided to ignore the advice and accept the peril. I would work hard to continue doing good surface science but also continue being involved in those other things that I valued in my life. For me it was an important choice. When the time came for the new grant application, I did have progress to report. Two new surface science papers had been published, and three more were accepted and in various stages of the publication process. These five papers demonstrated that the effort supported by the previous grant had been productive. The Program Director acknowledged that I had delivered on that promise. A new round of reviews resulted in three ratings: two of *excellent* and one of *very good*. The proposal was turned down.

I saw it as the end of that road. Frequently when a grant proposal is rejected, we see what we can learn from the reviewers' comments, think about ways to improve the proposal, and resubmit an improved version the following year. This time I could see no point in putting together a new proposal. There was no way I could hope to get any better ratings than this from reviewers on any proposal. I know, from reviewing proposals sent to me, that the line between my giving a rating of *very good* or *excellent* is fuzzy enough that I might not be consistent from one week to the next in using those ratings. There is inevitably a significant subjective component to the judgment. This was clearly a case where the NSF program director had made the decision, and unless I exhibited some dramatic burst of productivity over the next two or three years without NSF support, there was no chance of appeal.

Had I been treated unfairly? Probably not. The Program Director is in a bind. If the number of dollars to support research in his area were constant over a period of years, for him to be able to award a grant to a promising young scientist, he would have to terminate support for someone else whose research he has been supporting. Given inflation, the dollar cost of doing research is constantly increasing, and if total research dollars are constant, he must terminate more than one grant recipient for each new one started. My impression is that the dollar amount to support research in this area was actually decreasing, making the problem even more acute. He must support promising young scientists, eager to make their contributions, and to do it he must terminate support for older scientists. He doesn't have many options.

Some years ago I had made another choice that substantially reduced my options for support for my research. Prior to World War II there had been little government support for basic research. After the war some people saw it to be in the nation's interest to have some ongoing support for basic research, and the Office of Naval Research became an agency that supported a variety of fundamental research programs. My impression is that a number of scientists, in the generation before mine, thought that this agency did a good job in running the basic research program, making their judgments for support based primarily on the quality of the research rather than on its short-term applications. The ONR program became a model for government funding of fundamental research, and other military branches set up offices for such support. Later a new agency, the National Science Foundation, was established as the first government agency whose prime purpose was to support basic research in the sciences.

I have some strong personal reservations about being involved in military research. I would have difficulty in seeing my life's efforts directed to developing more effective ways of killing people, and I will not direct my efforts toward such a goal. But where do I draw the line when I live in a world where I acknowledge the need for police forces? How do I view my involvement with research that has applications to the military enterprise? It is difficult to find a consistent position; in fact, it is hard to think of developments that have no possible applications to military goals.

Suppose a psychologist or sociologist comes up with an effective strategy for conflict resolution in small groups. Such a development has to be a positive influence for our society; it would also be of considerable interest to the Navy, which must have significant problems with a ship's crew and the enforced togetherness it must experience. But concluding that a consistent position is impossible for a person who lives in the real world is different from saying that there are no choices one can make. This problem was brought home to me very early in my research career.

After I finished graduate school, I worked for a few months as a temporary, part-time employee in a laboratory associated with the University. The lab was involved with some interesting problems, most of them supported by grants from the military. I was hired to build an instrument that could look at a light source and simultaneously measure the intensity of the light at four different wavelengths: two in the visible, one in the ultraviolet, and one in the infrared. It would provide information with which we could characterize different types of light sources. I was familiar with the appropriate technology, and it was a straightforward task that I could manage in the short time I would be there. I could name a number of applications for which such an instrument would be useful. One of the obvious ones at the time, and the one that I suspected was the immediate motivation for the instrument, had to do with missiles that could be guided to attack jet aircraft.

The exhaust of a jet is a bright source of light that radiates energy in all parts of the spectrum but gives a large amount of radiation in the infrared, a region in which the radiation from the sky would be quite low. A "heat-seeking missile" is one that homes in on the infrared radiation of the jet. For every "measure" in this kind of military contest there is a "countermeasure." The obvious countermeasure here is for the plane, pursued by a heat-seeking missile, to eject some flares that are burning brightly enough to provide alternate targets to lure the missile away from the plane. But for every countermeasure there is also a counter-counter-measure, and so on—a chain without end.

A counter-countermeasure for the decoy flares is a detector on the missile that can distinguish between the radiation from the jet engine and that from the flare. That should not be hard to do. A small amount of inflammable material in the flare, by burning at a very high temperature, could produce an amount of infrared radiation as great as that from the jet exhaust. However, at that high temperature it should produce more visible light than the jet. A detector could distinguish between the two light sources by measuring the brightness of the radiation, both in the visible and in the infrared, and calculating the ratios of these two quantities. The higher ratio would reveal the "signature" of the decoy flare that would be obviously different from that of a jet engine.

I had not been told that the instrument I was building was a part of the development of such a counter-countermeasure. Although that application was obvious, so were a number of others that I felt more comfortable with. One afternoon another person working in the lab wandered into my work area with a cup of coffee in hand and started to talk about this problem of distinguishing a jet exhaust from a flare. If you were going to do it with the simplest system that used only two wavelengths, which wavelengths should you choose? If you knew the temperatures of the exhaust and of the flare, it would not be difficult to calculate which two wavelengths would give a ratio that would be the most different for the two sources. Did I want him to do the calculation? I really didn't want to talk about it; I didn't even want to *think* about it.

His question put the issue to me clearly, where, in fact, I had been trying to keep it blurry. If this really were the motivation for the project, then my half-hearted participation in it was an untenable approach. Either I signed on to the project and tried to make it successful—to make a missile that could more effectively destroy a jet plane—or I got out. Getting out was not a big deal; it was a short-term job and, as planned, I shortly moved on to a permanent job. However, after I left the Allis Chalmers Central Research Laboratories and went to the University of Wisconsin-Milwaukee, the question resurfaced.

Much of the support for basic research available to a faculty member in the physical sciences is provided by various military agencies. I would argue that if it is considered in the national interest for the government to support an infrastructure of basic research in the county's universities (and I think that it is), then the oversight of such money should be assigned to agencies, such as NSF, for whom such support is the primary agenda, rather than funneled through military organizations, where such support is always in danger of being skewed by the mission of the organization. This is not only the case for the Department of Defense but also for Agriculture, Mining, Commerce, and other agencies given responsibility for particular areas of our society. Let these agencies sponsor the research activities that are needed to support their assigned missions, but let the support of fundamental research be in charge of an agency, or agencies, for which such support is the primary responsibility.

This is not a very radical proposal. A number of countries have networks of laboratories that have a mission to support fundamental research, independent of the university system and of other government agencies. Examples include the system of Max Planck Laboratories spread throughout Germany, the CNRS (National Center for Scientific Research) Laboratories of France, the Academy of Sciences in a number of Eastern European countries, and the CSIRO (Commonwealth Scientific and Industrial Research Organization) Laboratories in Australia. The closest we come in this country to such a system are the National Laboratories that are generally centered around an experimental facility that is too expensive for any one institution to support.

In general we expect our research-oriented universities to perform the function of maintaining a national infrastructure of fundamental research and knowledge. This function gets lost in the budget-cutting debates that are taking place at both state and national levels today. More and more we hear state legislators claim that the function of public universities is to teach students, and if professors are not spending most of their hours in front of classes of students, they are getting away with something. In this mindset applied research may have some place, but research not directed toward solving an immediate, pressing problem of our society is an indulgence, and a faculty member wasting time studying and learning about new developments in science that are not directly related to his or her "function" is perhaps not to be tolerated in difficult times. The dual mission of the universities in our country is not well understood.

My opinion on the organization for science in the country aside, the facts of life for a university researcher are as they are. The Department of Defense is a major source of funds for basic research. Some of my friends with such support point out that they are doing the same thing they would be doing if NSF or the PTA were paying the bill. I have the concern that if I am not willing to point out the implications of my work for the mission of the military organization paying the bills, then I am in an unsatisfactory position.

The question is where to draw the line. I am not willing to work on weapons development at one end of the spectrum of choices. On the other end I am willing to work on understanding processes that I know may be applied to ends over which I have no control. Between the No and the Yes lies a continuum of choices, with no clear place to draw a logically consistent line. The place I drew my line was not to accept funds for my research from any military agency. It was a decision that significantly limited my options for research support.

After my NSF support ended, I continued surface science research on a reduced scale. I got enough money from the Petroleum Research Fund to (sometimes) support one graduate student and pursue projects that required no new equipment or costly procedures. Interesting results came out of that effort, but the game was changed.

> **In preparation for the "Discussion Group" I am trying to think how to answer the question: "What have I learned?" I keep thinking about choices. What other choices have I consciously made that have shaped my career? Often the choices have to do with how I spend my time.**

I have been ambitious to do good research, but I also have a sense of wanting to invest time in my teaching and in the interactions with students and colleagues that affect the way my department and my university operate. How much time do I have to do research? It is a slippery question. Count up the hours that go into preparation for each hour of lecture in class, add on the hours to put together and grade significant exams, include time talking with students either during formal office hours or informally, add in time for committee meetings and for preparation for the issues involved, and one might think that everything else is left for research. There are still a lot of time leaks. Where do I count the time spent talking to the local Astronomy Club, or to a high school class, or to the Rotary Club? What about departmental colloquia and seminars? And what about the phone calls from people from the community who have questions about physics, or reporters who have questions about physics (and a ten o'clock deadline), or people from small or large businesses who have technical questions that I might be able to answer?

Of the time that gets listed under the heading of research, a lot of it is background time, time that must be spent just to keep me in the position to be able to do research. I count about twenty scientific publications that arrive in my mail each month that I scan, obviously not reading all but looking at some articles in each. Many more that I need to look at arrive at the university library. Writing grant proposals and articles for publication takes considerable time, and if one is a part of the scientific community, peer-reviewing the grant proposals and papers of others is a part of the job as well.

The time actually spent *doing* research usually doesn't start until the first forty or fifty hours of the week are spent on other things. It is easy to conclude that by putting in just a few more hours per week, I could double the actual time I spend doing research. And here is the hard decision. Some people may look for activities to "kill time," but that is not my problem. If I put more time on one part of my life, it has to be taken away from some other part. Most of us prepare lectures and read the scientific journals at home in the evening. Some colleagues say that Saturday morning is the one time they can work in the lab with few interruptions.

My family is an important part of my life, and in the competition for my time, they have ranked high on the priority list. I made the decision to keep Saturdays for life-maintenance and family activities. Frequently, with small children, we would plan on Saturday morning to do jobs (mow the lawn, fix the leaky faucet, put in the storm windows . . .) and Saturday afternoon to do something together as a family.

However, in the equation of my life, it is true that more time spent with family means less time spent on research. It's a choice.

The problem with an aphorism, even if it contains the distilled essence of great experience and summarizes great understanding, is that it is only understood by someone who has gone through most of that experience and has struggled with the understanding. It may summarize an insight, but it can't teach that insight to someone who doesn't already almost understand it.

Oh, well, I have to respond somehow. Choices about how to spend time seem to have taken a lot of attention over my adult life. Here goes.

Comments about TIME:

I look at the different parts of my life, which includes a variety of professional interests and ambitions, a variety of personal interests and ambitions, and a variety of significant relationships with spouse, kids, and friends. There is never enough time to develop all the different parts of those iterests and relationships to what they could be.

INSIGHT #1. I only get rewards or satisfactions from those parts of my life on which I spend some time.

INSIGHT #2. When I am using all the time there is, "trying harder" doesn't solve anything. My life is going to be an interlocking set of compromises, where expanding the time spent in one area reduces the time spent in another area, and the best I can hope for is a set of compromises that brings me some long term satisfaction in the balance.

INSIGHT #137. Time flies like an arrow. Fruit flies like a banana.

Chapter Fourteen

BASIC RESEARCH

It has been ten days since I sent the article to the bee-keeping journal. Flottum must have read it by now; I wonder how he reacted to my criticism of his editorials. I don't know the man. He might try to pick out a few sentences, put them together to make me sound like a nut, and publish it as a Letter to the Editor. I tried to forestall that possibility by telling him in the letter that if he did any substantial editing of the piece, I wanted to approve it before it was published. Or he might reject the whole thing, saying that the discussion is not appropriate for his journal. The thing to do is to call him and find out what he is thinking. If he suggests drastically reducing it in length, maybe I'll suggest—more like, threaten—to send it to the rival beekeeping magazine to see if they want to publish it. I guess the thing to do is give him a call.

Kim Flottum is the editor of one of the two magazines widely read by beekeepers. I had a strong disagreement with his editorial in the November 1995 issue of *Bee Culture*. He may have intended it simply as a criticism of scientists who don't explain their work to the public, but it sounded to me like a general assault on the role of basic research. Then, in the December issue, he repeated some of his charges, lambasting academic scientists who do their "useless" research. He wrote that he was disappointed, though not surprised, that not any of them had bothered to defend their behavior. That one got to me. I suspected that if I did not write a rebuttal to those editorials, it might be that no one else would reply, either.

I was recuperating from foot surgery and had limited mobility. Although I didn't have any ambitions to be known in the beekeeping community, it was a reasonable time for me to write a response, and I decided to do it. I needed to come up with an example showing where basic research produced some unanticipated benefit to beekeeping. The example would most likely come from the area of biology, which is not my strong suit.

John Greenler, my son-in-law, with his background in molecular biology, suggested that I cite the application of a process for replicating DNA to studying the genetics of bees. That provided the example that could serve as the hook for the argument. He also mentioned that the enzyme used in this replicating process comes from bacteria that were found at places in the deep ocean where extremely hot water spews forth from cracks in the ocean floor. I was able to pick the brains of colleagues in the biological sciences who worked with this replication process and some who knew about deep-ocean hot vents. I spent a lot of time working over the article before I was satisfied with it, and this is what I finally sent to Editor Flottum:

RESEARCH IN BEE CULTURE
Robert Greenler

Kim Flottum's editorial in the November *Bee Culture* was prompted by the retirement (sort of) of Roger Morse from his position as Professor of Apiculture at Cornell University. The event led the editor to comment on his perception of the contributions (and lack of contributions) to beekeeping practice by academic research scientists, Morse being an exception to his generally poor opinion of this group of people. He expressed some strong opinions on a subject that has long been of concern to me, but the thing that prompted me to organize my thoughts on paper was his December editorial where he wrote:

> Recently I discussed the problems associated with getting information generated by public-funded

academic studies into the hands of the people who not only can use the information, but are the ones who helped pay for it. I accused these people, these academic types, of arrogance, of stupidity, and indifference. I see no reason to change my mind, nor have I had any, repeat any, come to defend their behavior ... I am not surprised. Disappointed yes. Surprised, no.

I must admit to being one of these academic types, whose work has received funding from public agencies, and although I agree with some of the editor's opinions in this matter, I would like to express a different point of view. Perhaps it is appropriate for me to start by mentioning two qualifications I have for joining this discussion.

I have been a small-time beekeeper for over a half century, with a few years off in my early adult years. I don't exactly know when I started beekeeping, because I can't remember just when I started going with my father to care for the 150 to 200 colonies that he kept in eight or ten different locations in northwestern Ohio. For him, beekeeping was obviously a hobby that got out of control and became a part-time business. It fit rather well with his other business of school-teaching, requiring the most time when school was out. He was an active participant in state beekeeping meetings and was one of the charter members of an Ohio honey-marketing cooperative. I went with him to work the bees as early as I can remember and, by the time I was 10 or 12, I could do my share as we worked together. I would like to discuss the influence of that shared activity on my life—but that may be the subject of another article, not this one.

My second qualification for some opinions on the role of research in bee culture is that I have been involved in research over the past 40 years—not in apiculture, but in several areas in physics. Although my research activity may seem unrelated to beekeeping, I believe there are questions concerning the relevance of research to the ordinary citizen that are common to all the sciences.

In support of Kim Flottum's argument, I have often argued

with my colleagues that a reasonable part of a professional scientist's obligation is an effort to explain the workings of science to nonscientists. This was a part of my motivation in starting and running a series of public programs at the University of Wisconsin-Milwaukee. The series, called *The Science Bag*, is now in its 23rd year and has had, to date, a cumulative attendance of over 105,000 people. It is significant that 54 different faculty members have contributed from one to twenty different programs to this long-running series.

A concern for sharing science with the public was also part of my motivation for writing a book, *Rainbows, Halos, and Glories*. This book discusses beautiful optical effects of the sky with a nonmathematical treatment intended to be accessible to people who are curious about the world around us but who don't have the background of a scientist. The book is still in print 15 years after its first publication, and I take pleasure in the letters about it that arrive nearly every week. They come from people who have just discovered the book and have enjoyed it to the point of writing me a letter to tell me so—and also to share an effect, perhaps with a photo, of something interesting they have seen.

So I am very interested in sharing the insights and pleasures of science with others. On the other hand, there is an area of research that I have worked on for years with support from the National Science Foundation that I don't talk about in my *Science Bag* presentations. Although I've published dozens of papers from this work in scientific journals, I have seldom written about it in articles for the public. The reason is not an arrogance or indifference to the public and, although the public has supported this work, I do not think they have been cheated in the transaction. To explain that idea, I will try to describe the kind of research I am talking about.

It might help clarify the discussion by describing two kinds of approaches to research. The most familiar approach is that of applied research, where effort is directed toward solving a specific problem. A less-well understood approach is that of fundamental research or basic research where the effort is invested to understand the workings of nature, rather than to solve a specific, identified problem. It is not that such research has no identified goals, but that the goals are to develop an understanding in a particular scientific area, without a precise knowledge of where that understanding will lead. The work that I will try to describe is an example of basic research.

I study the structure of molecules that are stuck on metal surfaces. My students and I have developed some techniques that can yield detailed pictures of how an isolated molecule can approach a surface, orient itself, possibly break into two fragments, and form bonds between certain atoms in the molecule and certain metal atoms in the surface. As new molecules arrive, we can understand how they interact with those already attached and either arrange themselves in patterns of the surface or react with the fragments of molecules sitting there. The tools and techniques that we use to get this kind of information are not familiar to nonscientists, and a person has to have a lot of persistence to acquire sufficient background to enable him or her to understand what the experiments reveal about these molecules stuck on the surface. An obvious question is, "Who cares?"

Who cares, indeed, whether a carbon monoxide molecule attaches to a platinum atom through the carbon atom or through the oxygen atom and whether it stands up or lays down on the surface? It doesn't appear to make much difference in the life of an ordinary citizen, and despite my interest in sharing science with the public, I find it difficult to write a magazine article about this work that will catch a reader's interest. Who, then, is interested in what we find out about this molecular dance that we study?

The consumer for the information we develop may be a theoretical physicist or chemist, more skilled in mathematics than I, who constructs an abstract model to represent the effects we have discovered. Such a contribution might seem to move the science even further away from solving problems in the real world. On the other hand, another one who reads my papers may be a catalytic chemist who is trying to develop a more efficient catalyst to make gasoline, or to produce antifreeze or countless other chemical products that we use, or to reduce noxious gases that result from incomplete combustion of fuels used in automobiles.

Or the reader may be the physicist or chemical engineer who is trying to develop a catalyst that will enable us to use the energy of sunlight to split water molecules into hydrogen and oxygen. Success in that venture could conceivably enable us to use sunlight to provide hydrogen as a source of usable fuel for the energy needs of our society and offer a new approach to solving the energy problems that affect all parts of the world community. Or the reader may be the engineer who is looking at the effect of layers only one molecule thick on the performance of smaller and smaller circuits on computer chips.

The point of this personal story is to question the unstated assumption behind Kim Flottum's criticism of academic research that if the results of the research can't be explained and are not useful to the person on the street, then that person, whose taxes supported the research, is being bilked. I think that the debate of the value of basic research versus applied research is very much the same in all the sciences, but let me try to develop an example more closely related to beekeeping.

My biologist friends talk about a technique called the polymerase chain reaction (PCR). As I understand it, with this technique they can use an enzyme to mark the two ends of a particular strip that is contained in a long DNA spiral, and then replicate that strip, multiplying the quantity of that DNA up to a billion-fold in a test tube. Using this technique, from a minute sample they can produce enough identical material to allow a variety of investigations. As it has developed, these investigations have led to two types of applications. One is the now-familiar use of DNA in forensic medicine, for example, identifying the source of a small trace of blood found at the scene of a crime. The other is to identify the genetic background of an individual, whether it be plant or animal. Each individual has its own unique DNA, and the offspring carries in its DNA information about both of its parents, and their parents, and their parents. . . .

In some universities work with this technique might be done in the same department that house the entomologists, among whom there might be a someone studying the biology of bees. For a person interested in bee culture, a few years ago it would be easy to assume that the guy playing with PCR had nothing to contribute to his interest. On the other hand, the question of the spread of the African bees into our southern states and the effect of their interbreeding with local bee poulations might be of considerable interest to him. How does he view the development if the entomologist discovers that his colleague's PCR techniques could be used to trace the northern spread of African bees, and, furthermore, trace the genetic influence of this stock on a local population as more and more interbreeding takes place? (See Mark Winston's discussion "Hybrid Bees" in the June 1995 *Bee Culture*.)

There is another interesting twist behind this development of the PCR technique. Where did it come from? It came from a most unlikely source. The key to the process is an enzyme that can stand high temperatures. The original enzymes used in this process came from bacteria that grew in hot springs in Yellowstone Park. Another enzyme that has some additional advantages for this technique comes from bacteria that were discovered deep in the ocean at places where the earth's molten interior comes close enough to the ocean floor to produce hot springs that spew forth mineral-rich water with temperatures up to 700 degrees Fahrenheit. At great-enough depths the pressure of the water is so high that it can be this hot without boiling. It was an amazing discovery that, under extremes of temperature and pressure, at depths to which no sunlight can penetrate, there are many living things. Around these deep-ocean hot vents there are rich colonies of life, including varieties of fish, crabs, mussels, clams, and worms, all based on bacteria that can thrive in regions near the vents where the water temperature is up to 280 degrees Fahrenheit. This is a life-supporting environment that is totally alien to any we knew before. These conditions are as different from what we were familiar with as the conditions we might expect to find on another planet.

The connection with the PCR technique is that bacteria found at these hot vents contain enzymes that can survive high temperatures, temperatures that would destroy most of the enzymes that we previously knew. One of the uses found for these high-temperature enzymes is to enable biologists to neatly replicate a section of DNA. This is the PCR technique that will work only at temperatures that will kill other enzymes.

Suppose, at the time this newly discovered, deep-ocean, hot-vent environment was being explored, someone, in an attempt to justify the exploration, was trying to predict the consequences of the insight that could come from the investigation. It is unthinkable that they would have suggested that it might help answer questions about the economic impact of the African bee on the U.S. honey industry. And yet, this is the kind of story that so often comes out of basic research, directed at new understanding with no clear vision as to where it will lead.

To bring the discussion back home, even the Roger Morses and Mark Winstons, who write for this journal and contribute so much to understanding and progress in bee culture, need information on which to base their work. I'm sure that they read the journals that we beekeepers can't understand. In his article "Payback Time" in the April 1995 *Bee Culture* Mark Winston does a calculation to justify the direct value of his work to taxpayers but he does not mention the value that he gets from people whose work is more fundamental than his own.

These scientists are part of a web of activity that spans the gamut from basic investigations, whose relevance is not obvious, to the very applied research questions aimed at solving specific problems in our everyday lives. I believe it is a mistaken short-range strategy that suggests that we can have the benefits of this web of research by eliminating all but the last step. It may well be that there is a shortage of Roger Morses and Mark Winstons—that we need more people to apply the insights of basic investigations to help solve our everyday beekeeping problems—but we should also value the essential contributions behind that last step in the research process.

There's no use to put it off any longer—I'll make the call. "Hello, Kim Flottum? This is Robert Greenler. If you've had the time to look at the article I sent you recently, I'm interested in your reaction to it."

(Pause—seemed to me to be a long pause).

"Well, yes, I've just read it. I'll publish it as a guest editorial in the March issue, and I won't change a word."

I realize that I was prepared for almost any answer but that one.

Chapter Fifteen

THE OPTICAL SOCIETY OF AMERICA

"There are strongly held views on both sides of this question. It has been much discussed, and we need to come to some decision today. I propose that we go around the table and give each person the opportunity to express himself or herself fully without being interrupted—unless it is for a matter of clarification. You don't need to counter another person's argument because you will have an uninterrupted time to present your own views. After going around the table once, each person will have another turn to respond to anything that has been brought up. I consider it my role in this discussion to help facilitate a decision, and so I will not take a position and will not vote. Are we ready?"

The question was whether or not the Optical Society of America should form a federation with the SPIE, the International Society of Optical Engineering.

This was the most difficult question that we had to deal with at the annual board meeting of the Optical Society in the year when I was president. The decision itself may not have been the most important thing we had to deal with, but I was very concerned over the possible fallout from the decision.

In 1987 these were the two largest optical scientific and engineering groups in the world, and they had very different cultures. The Optical

Society of America was a membership-driven organization that arranged meetings so that the engineer/scientist members could get together to tell others about their work. The eight journals published by the Optical Society were peer-reviewed, and the positions of editor, associate editor, and reviewer were mostly volunteer. The large general meeting, the smaller, topical meetings organized in new, rapidly developing scientific areas, and the scientific journals were all very important in the professional lives of Optical Society members.

In contrast, SPIE was organized from the top down; SPIE members tended to be less involved in running their society. The organizations could operate differently because, for engineers, publishing papers and giving talks at technical meetings does not have as much importance as it does for scientists. SPIE meetings were arranged so that experts could acquaint members with new developments and give review talks about areas of technology for members who needed the information. SPIE's emphasis was to provide educational services for its members rather than to be an agent of cooperative information exchange. Although there were no clearly defined boundaries, SPIE tended to deal with engineering applications and the Optical Society with more fundamental science.

The board of directors of the Optical Society was to decide on a proposed federation that would combine some of the activities of these two groups. Different members of the board held strong feelings, both for and against the federation. It seemed to me that the harmonious operation of our organization could be affected by the decision, and that the possible loss of harmony might well be more significant than the decision itself, so it was important for someone to pay very careful attention to the process by which the decision was reached. On this day, that was my job. How on earth had I had gotten myself into such a position? As I moved through my academic career, I had never felt any aspirations to become president of this (or any) scientific society, but here I was.

First, let me describe more completely the nature of the Optical Society of America. The scientific focus of the organization is considerably broader than its name suggests to most nonscientists. (I've heard enough variations of the joke, "If you're the president of the Optical Society, can you tell me what's wrong with my eyeglasses?" to last for a while.) More complicated optical instruments may also come to mind, but maybe not much else. Actually, the Society deals with all the areas concerning the nature of light itself or involving the interaction of light with matter. This includes spectroscopy (in the visible, ultraviolet, X-ray, and infrared regions), fiber optics, lasers, holography, optical computing, optical data storage, image recording and processing, vision, and, over the past three decades, a rapidly increasing list of new areas that can be probed and understood by optical methods.

If I try to trace the winding path that led me to the presidency of this organization, I think back to my color laboratory next to the barn in West Unity and my early fascination with the rainbow. What other signs can I find to mark the path? Where else was I fascinated by things optical, a fascination that led me, unseeing, into this part of my career? I will try to identify some of the markers.

When I was a small child we went, a few times a year, to visit friends of my parents in the small town of Green Springs, Ohio, where my father had taught school before I was born. Though this couple was half a generation older, their relationship to my parents was indicated by their honorary aunt-and-uncle status for me and my sisters. One day, apropos of nothing I recall, I mentioned to my father that there was something special about looking out of the window next to Uncle Al's reading chair. He looked at me in a kind of funny way and asked what I meant. I didn't really know what made that window so special, but somehow everything seemed so clear when I looked out that window, across the broad lawn to the tree-lined streets of Green Springs.

By some chance my father happened to know that Uncle Al had installed a piece of plate glass in that window, next to the chair from which he viewed the comings and goings of the town. Ordinary window glass has a certain amount of waviness, producing some distortion of the scene viewed through it. Plate glass is ground and polished to be quite flat. My father found it interesting that without any discussion about the window, and without knowing anything about the cause, I had apparently noticed the lack of distortion introduced by the plate-glass window.

I thought of that incident many years later when I recognized a habit I had developed, without thinking, in the locker room of the university gym. After showering and getting dressed at my locker, I would go to a mirror to comb my hair. But I would pass up the mirror most convenient to my locker and use another, a few steps farther away. I realized that the flatness of the mirror that I used was superior to the nearer one, and apparently the aesthetic advantage was worth the few steps to me.

When I was in the eighth or ninth grade, I discovered kaleidoscopes, and I continued building and playing with them through high school. I understood that if you laid two mirrors together along their long edge and tilted them apart in a V, you could see multiple images of an object placed at the far end of the mirrors. I figured out that you saw, directly, a toothpick, for example, crossing the pie-shaped area defined by the far ends of the mirrors. If you looked a bit to the left, you saw an image of the toothpick reflected in the left mirror. If you looked farther to the left, you saw another image, and after a while I understood how that happened. A line of sight drawn (backward) from your eye to the toothpick would reflect first off the left mirror and then off the right mirror and then to the toothpick.

Each successive image in the rosette required one more reflection than the previous image. Looking to the right, you also saw a series of pie-shaped images. If you picked the angles between the mirrors just right, then the images on the far side of the pattern would exactly match up. If the angle between the mirrors were ninety degrees, then there would be four segments to the pattern; if it were forty-five degrees, there would be eight segments; if it were thirty degrees, twelve segments. I was delighted to realize that there was a general expression; if you wanted N segments (where N could be any whole number), the desired angle between the mirrors was 360/N degrees.

Actually, when you look at the pattern formed by that toothpick running diagonally across the pie-shaped segment of the kaleidoscope field—and all of its mirror images—you are most aware of the star shape of the pattern. What strikes you more than the number of segments in the pattern is the number of points on the star. Since it takes two segments to produce one point on the star, we can modify the expression for the mirror angle to get a star with P points. It is 360/2P. So if we should want to get a six-pointed star pattern, we need to set the mirrors at an angle of thirty degrees to each other. I remember seeing somewhere an article about kaleidoscopes that gave that formula, and it was exciting to me that I could understand what it meant.

During that time I made a variety of kaleidoscopes, varying from large to small. The smallest was built in a little tube that had contained bouillon cubes and was about three inches long. My young eyes could focus on the miniature pattern only three inches from my eye, but none of the adults to whom I showed it could see anything. Now I know that a simple lens put over the viewing hole would solve the problem; at the time I neither understood what kind of lens I needed nor did I have any idea where one might be obtained. I wasn't yet that far along the optics path.

I did make one invention with the kaleidoscope. If I set the two mirrors at sixty degrees and then added a third mirror along the open side of the V, something very interesting happened to the pattern: instead of being a rosette, the pattern extended in all directions. The result is like a tile pattern that completely covers a two-dimensional plane. Although I "invented" the device, it had been known to others for a long time; I was not the first nor, I'm sure, the last person to invent it.

Another marker along the path occurred when I was in college and discovered the Edmund Salvage Company, a source of cheap, war-surplus optics. (That is where I could have gotten the lens for my mini kaleidoscope.) The company has upgraded its image and product line, and now goes by the name Edmund Scientific Company. With the help of Edmund Salvage, I built a 35-mm slide projector, which, at the time, seemed to me to be a significant achievement. An echo of that project appeared only recently.

Barbara and I were to spend some time with Ray and Ellie Newell at our cabin. I phoned them beforehand to suggest that they bring along slides of our early canoe and camping trips, and I would provide the slide projector. The only thing that made the suggestion a little surprising is that we have no electricity at the cabin. I told them that I would bring along a gasoline-powered projector. On the evening of the showing, I brought out the insides of a store-bought slide projector that had fallen on hard times (with broken condensing lenses and mechanical difficulties). I had modified it with a hacksaw by sawing off the structure that supported the projection bulb and some of the condensing lenses.

With these changes a gasoline lantern could be placed close enough so that the glowing mantle of the lantern could be imaged directly onto the slide, producing a reasonable illumination for projecting the slide on the sheet hung from the sleeping balcony. How well did it work? At first we were all quite impressed that it worked at all; after that we were impressed that it worked well enough that we could, indeed, view the slides, even though they weren't very bright.

If I had been intending all along to follow a career in optics, the move to go to the University of Rochester would have been a logical choice. The Institute of Optics at Rochester was one of the world's leading institutions in optical science and engineering. But the path that led in that direction also had a number or random twists and turns.

Why Rochester? I was interested in science; I preferred a medium-sized school to a large school; and I had seen some description that fixed in my mind, without any particular rational basis, that it would be an exciting place. I would need some financial aid to go there, and I knew that the University had some Bausch and Lomb Scholarships. To apply for a scholarship one had to be the recipient of the Bausch and Lomb Science Medal in high school. We were now living in Toledo, and I was to receive that award from my school. My high-school principal told me that when the scholarship-application information came in, he would give it to me.

As spring vacation of my senior year approached, my friend, Dwayne, and I cooked up a plan. Neither of us had ever been to New York City. Given a whole week of vacation, we figured that we could hitchhike there and back and still have two or three days to see the city. We could sleep on the floor of the apartment of Dwayne's cousin who lived in New York, so that wouldn't cost us anything. I told my parents of our great plans and, although they didn't seem to fully share our enthusiasm, they didn't stop me from going. On the last day of classes before vacation, the principal told me in passing, "Oh, Greenler, that information from the University of Rochester is in. Stop by my office sometime and pick it up." I said I would do it right after vacation.

So we started thumbing our way down the road, our exact route to the big city being influenced by the direction of the rides that we happened to get. A long ride at the end of the first day landed us in Rochester. As long as we were there, why not go out to visit the campus before continuing to New York City? So when the Director of Admissions arrived at his office the next morning, he found two, quite unsophisticated boys sitting on the steps, waiting to tell him of their plans for the future.

I told him that I was to get the Bausch and Lomb medal and was going to apply for the scholarship so that I could come to the University of Rochester next year. I was aware that he asked several carefully phrased questions. After a few minutes of conversation, he said, "I'm afraid that your principal didn't do very well by you. The last letter he received from us pointed out that the scholarship applications were due, and we hadn't received any from his school." The deadline was now past, and, in fact, most of the scholarships had already been awarded.

I suspect that my naiveté was so obvious that he believed my story. He told me to fill out the application as soon as I got back and to send it marked to his attention. We went on to New York City, spent three days riding the subway, eating in automats, and seeing the sights, and got home safely. I completed the application and was notified that although all of their scholarships had been committed, I was listed as an alternate for a four-year tuition scholarship, and I would hear about that later. As a backup, I registered at the local university, where I could attend classes and live at home, but in July I received the letter from Rochester saying that I had a tuition scholarship.

The game of "What if?" is not an exercise in reality, but it is a game that is hard to resist playing. If the luck of the hitchhiker had not put us in Rochester that night, I assume that I would have sent in my late application and been told that I had missed the deadline and no scholarship aid was available. In that case, who knows?

Some years later, after I had acquired a slightly different view of the world, I asked my mother what she thought when we came up with our New York plans. She said that she had asked my father, "Can we possibly let them go?'" and his response had been, "I don't see how we can possibly refuse." As it turned out, the adventure served as a sort of "rite of passage" for me, proving to me something about my ability to cope with the world. Going with their blessing meant that they were a part of the celebration of its success when I returned. I am aware of how often it happens that kids, denied permission for any adventure by parents concerned for their safety, have to find more and more dangerous ways to prove something about themselves. I hoped that I would remember something of that experience when I came to deal with my own children.

I didn't major in optics at Rochester, I majored in physics, but I did have a number of contacts with the optics community there. Ray Newell, my senior-year roommate and lifelong friend, was an optics major, and I had a year-long course in optics that I found most interesting. One of the semesters was taught by Robert Hopkins, at that time Director of the Institute of Optics. He was perhaps the first of a series of professors who warped my path toward the Optical Society. He also became, for me, a part of a tradition in optics which, some years later, I realized was also one of my traditions.

A part of any tradition or culture is the collection of personal stories about the people involved. A story that I contribute to the collection comes from this class taught by Professor Hopkins. He came to class one day excited about some unusual slides he had just received that illustrated the different kinds of aberrations that appear in optical systems. Because this was the Institute of Optics, there was a slide projector permanently mounted on the wall of each classroom. Professor Hopkins (Hoppy, to the graduate students) talked as he moved over to the projector, inserted the slides, flipped the switch, and looked expectantly at the screen. The screen was filled with light—but no image.

He stopped talking, looked at the projector, and realized that it had no projection lens. He asked a student to run down to the next classroom and borrow the lens from the projector there. A few minutes later the student returned, shrugging his shoulders; the lenses were gone from all of the classroom projectors. Where, but in the Institute of Optics, would lenses be useful for so many things that they disappeared from the classroom projectors, probably to be built in to someone's experimental setup? We never did see the aberration slides, but the story about their nonshowing remains part of the lore.

Earlier I described how I picked Johns Hopkins University for graduate school. I was not, knowingly, on my way to the Optical Society or to a career in optics, but by going to Johns Hopkins, I became associated with a long tradition of optics and spectroscopy. After some time I found that it became part of my tradition and that my life became connected with the chain of individuals behind the tradition. Henry Roland, after whom the physics building was named, had been an early faculty member who had made the first precision diffraction gratings, elements that spread light out into its spectrum very effectively. Following Rowland's death in 1901 young R. W. Wood was appointed professor of experimental physics. Wood became a world-famous scientist who, along with his highly developed scientific intuition and his skill as an experimentalist, had a flair for the dramatic. His discoveries and innovations are spread all over the scientific landscape, but his areas of special expertise were in optics and spectroscopy. Dozens of "R .W. Wood stories" exist, but one will suffice to illustrate his approach to problem solving.

Wood bought an old farmstead at East Hampton on Long Island and built there a summer laboratory that became the site of many of his discoveries and inventions. In one of the barns he built a large spectrograph that could spread out the spectrum of sunlight to a remarkable degree. If we view the spectrum of light given off by the hot vapor of sodium with a small tabletop spectroscope, we can see a bright line of yellow light. With only a moderately good spectroscope, we can see that this spectral line is actually two, closely spaced lines. In the spectrum that Wood photographed with his large spectrograph these two "closely spaced" lines were five inches apart. Although he could only photograph a short segment of the spectrum at any one time, the complete spectrum spread out by his instrument would have extended over fifty feet.

The instrument had a forty-two-foot-long wooden tube about six inches in diameter through which the light traveled. Over the first winter and spring after it was built, spiders got into the tube and spun their webs. So before Wood could use it the second summer, he needed to clean the webs out of the tube. Most of us would think of probing the tube from each end with a rag fastened on a long stick, or perhaps figure how to get a string through the tube to pull a cleaning rag through. And perhaps Wood did think of these things, too; however, what he did was something else. He grabbed the family cat, which he inserted, with some little struggle, into one end of the tube and then covered the end of the tube behind the cat. The cat sat for a few moments in the darkness and then headed off to the patch of light—and freedom—forty-two feet away, taking the spider webs with her as she escaped into the barnyard. That was a "Wood solution" to the problem.

Actually, I have taken a number of ideas from Wood. My copy of his book, *Physical Optics*, first published in 1905 and later evolving through several editions, has the inside back cover filled with notes of things that I might look into, things suggested by Wood's writing. The model of the hot-desert mirage that I showed in Toronto was an adaptation of the demonstration that Wood developed as an instructor at the University of Wisconsin before he went to Johns Hopkins.

A. H. Pfund, a contemporary of Wood at Johns Hopkins, would have had a larger share of the world's fame if he had not lived and worked in similar areas and in the shadow of the flamboyant Wood. I once heard his private comment repeated, that Wood had beat him to the best things he ever attempted, but that at least he was going to outlive him. Alas, he was even upstaged in that ambition by Wood, who lived to the age of eighty-five.

When I was first a graduate student, Wood was still living and came in to his laboratory occasionally. But my strongest connection with the Johns Hopkins tradition in optics came through my association with John Strong, who had joined the Hopkins faculty a few years after Wood had officially retired. My connection started with a summer job—and with my growing interest in optical phenomena.

I had come across a little book by Samuel Tolansky on multiple-beam interferometry that described some new techniques for using the interference of light to examine the flatness of surfaces. Actually, it might be more accurate to say that Tolansky developed ways to measure small deviations from flatness. He used arrangements where fringes of light would appear like contour lines on a surface, and a little step or scratch on the surface would show up as a jog in the light fringe. With his techniques he could measure steps in a surface with a height considerably smaller than a wavelength of light; in the most favorable case he could see steps as small as 1/500 of the wavelength of the light he was using. He was pushing his technique to measure things with the dimensions of molecules. The ingenuity of his methods and the beauty of his results stirred my imagination, and I remember staying up most of a night to finish reading his book. I wondered if I couldn't find some excuse to try his methods.

I needed to think about a job for the coming summer. The previous summer I had worked in Socorro, New Mexico, on a thunderstorm research project. In another year I would probably be involved in a research project for my Ph.D. dissertation, and I could see the future pattern from other students a bit further along the path than I. Once I started on that project, whatever it would be, I wouldn't be taking any summers off for any other job, but would be working full time on that research for the two or three years required to finish it. This seemed a possible time to spend a last summer at my parents' home in Toledo, if I could get a good-enough job there.

I knew that John Strong served as a consultant for the Technical Center of Libbey-Owens-Ford Company in Toledo, and so I went to see him about the possibility of a job in the Technical Center Laboratories. I cannot remember now whether I suggested the possibility of studying glass surfaces with multiple-beam interferometry or whether I found out from him that the laboratory was interested in exploring the possibility. However the idea came up, he liked it, called up someone at the lab who also thought it was an interesting possibility, and I had a summer job.

Until I sat down to write the account of this incident, I didn't realize how it fit into the pattern of later career moves. I was going to a place to try to use a new technique, a place where there was no one else knowledgeable in the technique, and a place with no laboratory facilities to do the work. I didn't even have the vacuum system necessary to coat the glass samples with metal to increase their reflectivity. I was put in the laboratory under the loose supervision of a chemist who had some interest in the glass polishing process. We defined the project as a feasibility study to see whether multiple-beam interferometry could be a useful tool to study the surface of glass. The laboratory was interested in the project and was willing to get what I needed to carry it out, but because I was only going to be there for three months, it was useless to order anything that couldn't be delivered immediately. So, by necessity, the approach was to improvise.

The only thing that made the project at all feasible was that it did not require much equipment. The particular technique of Tolansky that I proposed to use was one that he called Fringes of Equal Chromatic Order. I needed a little spectrograph that could record a spectrum on film and a lamp that emitted a small point of light, both of which I was able to borrow from the Physics Department at the University of Toledo. The more difficult part was improvising a vacuum system in which I could deposit a highly reflecting metal film on the glass specimens. For this purpose we added a small deposition chamber to the chemist-type vacuum system in the lab where I was working. Anyone with experience in these matters would have seen that the tube connecting the chamber to the vacuum pumps was too small and too long to maintain an adequate vacuum in the chamber.

John Strong came on a consulting visit and at once saw the difficulty. He suggested a solution that, I suppose, saved the project. We connected, directly to the deposition chamber, a large glass tube filled with charcoal powder. I heated the charcoal for several hours while pumping on it with the best vacuum I could get from the inadequate vacuum system. This treatment drove off gases that were adsorbed on the surface of the charcoal. I then turned off the heat and closed a valve to isolate the system from the vacuum pumps. Next, the tube of charcoal was chilled with a container of very cold liquid nitrogen, and the cold, clean charcoal surface adsorbed gases so effectively that it acted as a vacuum pump. It was a good-enough pump to produce an adequate vacuum for the time it took me to metalize the surface of my samples.

Altogether this was an ingenious solution, achieved in only a few days, to a problem that might have taken significantly longer to solve. The project had to keep moving if, in three months, I was to have any chance of building the apparatus, developing experimental techniques, and getting any results.

I did get all of the elements together and working so that, on a photographic plate, I could record the wiggly lines that gave a depth contour along an imaginary path traced across the glass surface. I could interpret these lines to give the depth and shape of irregularities on the glass surface. From the factory production lines I obtained samples of glass from various stages in the polishing process, and I also obtained a series of samples polished on a small machine in the laboratory. The Fringes of Equal Chromatic Order in my photographs showed the changes in the depths and shape contours of the surface features as the polishing proceeded.

At first I was tempted to think of these features as the pits left over from the grinding operation, but the appearance was deceiving. The magnification of the depth features on my wiggly lines was typically three hundred times greater than the magnification across the surface. What looked like pits were really very shallow depressions, with depths only about a thousandth of their diameter, and the depths of these features decreased only slowly as glass was removed by polishing. This kind of information was of interest to people who were trying to get a theoretical understanding of the glass-polishing process.

Glassmaking is an ancient art, and the polishing of glass surfaces is a technology that goes back a few centuries. But at the time I was doing these experiments, there was no agreement on the basic mechanism of the polishing process. Some theories considered the polishing process to be one in which the polishing particles removed glass like little planes, shaving away the surface.

Still other theories considered the glass to flow under the localized pressure of the particles, the polishing process being one in which the surface was "smoothed out" rather than being planed away. Another theory proposed that there was a chemical action that was significant in the process of glass removal. Isn't it strange that there was this lack of basic understanding of a process that was so important commercially and that had been used for so long?

Actually, I think there is a connection between the lack of basic understanding and the antiquity of the process. The scientific understanding developed slowly because the polishing of glass surfaces had developed so successfully as an ancient, empirical art. The traditions in such an industry are the traditions of techniques passed down from practitioner to apprentice. A scientific evaluation of techniques and even an openness to try new techniques develops only slowly among such traditions.

In the last couple of weeks on that project I made some microscopic measurements of grinding-pit sizes and determined the rate at which the pits disappeared as glass was removed by polishing. I did a mathematical analysis to relate this data to some other measurements of the total surface area of these samples. I wrote a report on my project, wrote another memo on the last little project and its analysis, and waved good-bye to the laboratory.

Sometime later one of the senior scientists from the lab arranged to talk with me at a scientific meeting, saying that he wanted to discuss the memo. He had gone through my mathematical derivation very carefully and thought that at one point I had made a mistake in the interpretation. As we looked at it together, it became clear that he was correct and that I had gotten it wrong. I was very embarrassed to have made the mistake. But his interest in the matter was not that I had gotten it wrong, but rather that to get it right we had only to make this change—and then we had the correct interpretation.

As I think about it at a much later time, the real significance of that conversation is that it showed that he was interested enough in the results of my project to spend the time going over the report and memo in detail to understand what I had done. It was a compliment. At the time it was also a lesson in humility.

I think there is an appropriate balance between humility and self-confidence, however. The two qualities may seem contradictory, but some of the people I admire most combine generous amounts of both characteristics. During the course of that summer at the Libbey-Owens-Ford Technical Center there was an incident that immediately did something for my self-confidence. That incident taught me something that was very important to me at the time and that I have also found to be important to many students starting to work on research.

I had been going to school for eighteen years. It seemed to me that everything I learned from a textbook was probably a simplified version of something that actually was more complicated. In addition, the person teaching each of the courses I took knew much more about it than I did. It was easy to get the impression that any "real" scientist knew much more about any given subject than I did. But here was a surprise. Something that I knew casually was both unknown and of significance to a Ph.D. engineer who also worked in the Technical Center. Since the evidence indicated that he was a competent fellow, the conclusion must be that I had picked up some useful information that not everyone knew. That insight was quite self-affirming to me.

Howard, who had a Ph.D. in Ceramics Engineering from the University of Illinois, had the reputation of being a competent problem solver and a good engineer. He was involved in studying the properties of glass and had formulated some new kinds of glasses, one of which had an unusually high index of refraction. The index of refraction is a measure of how much a ray of light is bent (refracted) when it enters the material, and it is an important characteristic of a glass.

The lab had a standard instrument for measuring the index of refraction (not surprisingly called a refractometer), but it didn't work for this specimen. To measure the index of refraction of a glass sample, one would grind and polish a flat face on the sample and put it in contact with a reference glass block on the refractometer. The measurement was made by illuminating the boundary and measuring the extreme angle for light emerging from the reference block. The principle on which the instrument operated depended on the reference block having a higher index of refraction than the sample being measured. Normally this was not a problem, but the new glass had an index higher than the reference block and, hence, could not be measured.

Howard understood why it didn't work, and he asked me if I knew how he might measure the high index. Nothing clever came to my mind, but I said that if he had a prism made of the glass, he could put it on the table of a spectroscope and, by measuring how the light was refracted by the prism, determine its index of refraction. He said that he could have someone manufacture a prism of the glass, and he did have access to an appropriate spectroscope. A convenient and accurate version of this measurement is to measure a quantity called the minimum angle of deviation. Once you have this minimum angle of deviation and the angle between the faces of the prism, you can calculate the index.

When Howard asked if I would be willing to help with the measurement, of course I agreed to help if there were a problem, but it is a straightforward measurement, and I gave him a reference to a textbook that described it. A couple of weeks later he came back to me. He had a sixty-degree prism of the experimental glass and had set up the spectrometer, but he could not get the procedure to work. He asked if I would be willing to take a look. After looking, I saw why it wasn't working, and I realized that it was due to my negligence.

In going through a prism, light changes the direction in which it is traveling. The angle by which it changes direction is called the angle of deviation. If you increase the angle of the prism, for example from fifty to sixty degrees, you increase the angle of deviation. However, there is a limit; if you make the prism angle too big, the light cannot emerge from the second face of the prism but gets totally reflected back inside the prism. For a glass with a typical index of refraction, this limiting prism angle is around eighty degrees, and so a sixty-degree prism of such a glass works well.

But this limiting angle decreases as the index of refraction increases, and the index of this experimental glass was so high that the limiting prism angle was just about sixty degrees, the angle of the prism Howard was trying to use. In fact, I could see that the red part of the spectrum could get though the prism and the blue part could not. You can understand that observation if you realize that the prism has a higher index of refraction for blue light than for red. It is that variation of the index with color that spreads the light out into a beautiful spectrum when it goes through the prism—or into a beautiful rainbow when it goes through a raindrop.

Although Howard had told me that the index of refraction of his experimental glass was very high, it never occurred to me that it might be so high that a sixty-degree prism made from it would not transmit light. I felt a bit sheepish for not thinking of that possibility, but his reaction was one of relief to understand the problem. The solution was simple: he had a new prism made with a thirty-degree angle, and I helped him do what was then a simple measurement to determine the remarkably high index of his new glass. Howard was pleased and grateful for my help, and I received a boost in self-confidence.

The summer at the laboratory of the glass company was a good experience and gave me the confidence that I might be able to do some respectable research. I arranged to do my thesis research with John

Strong and in that process moved directly into the tradition of optics at Johns Hopkins. Although I talk about "the tradition," no doubt different people each perceive a somewhat different tradition. A clear example of a different perception comes to my mind with an image of one of the maintenance men at the university.

Before we moved into John Strong's laboratory space in a new building adjacent to Rowland Hall, I occupied, for a few months, what had been Professor Pfund's laboratory. It was next door to the laboratory that had been used for half a century by Professor Wood, and to which he still occasionally came. One afternoon, as I was working in the laboratory, I looked up to see a man standing in the doorway, his thumbs stuck in the straps of his white painters' overalls, surveying the room and its jumbled contents. I would guess that he was close to sixty years old and had been painting rooms in the university for many years. "Well," he said as he looked over the room, "the old man would never let me in here when he was alive, but as soon as you move out, I'm finally going to paint it." He seemed to make this pronouncement with some satisfaction. And then he added, with the calm certainty of a man who knows he is going to accomplish the things he sets out to accomplish, "And one of these days, I'm even going to paint that one (indicating with his thumb Wood's lab next door), too." That maintenance man is also a part of the tradition.

Over his long and varied career John Strong did many things that caught the interest of the scientific community. As a postdoctoral fellow he developed a method of making mirrors by depositing a thin layer of aluminum on a polished glass surface. Immediately the aluminum film was seen as a much better coating for telescope mirrors than the thin silver films used previously. Over a period of months a silver surface tarnishes and its reflectivity drops; then the coating must be removed and the mirror resilvered. The aluminum films last for years without losing their very high reflectivity. Strong produced small mirrors, then larger and larger mirrors for telescopes, until he coated the one-hundred-inch-diameter mirror for the telescope on Mount Wilson. Later, when the Mount Palomar two-hundred-inch telescope was built, he was called on to supervise the coating of what was then the largest telescope mirror in the world. Today when we refer to an optical surface that has been "silvered," it almost invariably will really have been "aluminized."

John Strong also studied the atmospheres of planets with a telescope lifted by a large balloon above most of the earth's atmosphere. He made innovative changes in the way diffraction gratings are ruled and found ways to apply many of his instrumental innovations to problems in the study of the earth's atmosphere and to astronomy.

I once heard him comment that he had "observing time" on a number of the big telescopes around the country that he had not requested and didn't need. His explanation was that observational astronomers organize their careers to earn enough brownie points to get awarded precious observing time on the good telescopes. The time using the instruments is the payoff for a lot of other activity. He claimed that this mindset is so strong that the people who allot telescope time just assume that this is the motivation for anyone who produces innovative improvements in telescopes or telescope instrumentation. As a result of his very significant contributions in this area, he was rewarded with time that he had no use for. One of his students, Bill Sinton, did use the Palomar telescope to get the infrared spectrum of the atmosphere of Venus. I'd say that it is a pretty heady experience to be able, as a graduate student, to use the world's best telescope in your research.

It is difficult for me to sort out the many ways in which John Strong influenced my life and career, but two things come clearly to mind. There are scientists whose specialty is in knowing and understanding everything that has been published in a wide field. These people are valuable colleagues and, of course, may be productive scientists. But it is not always the people who know the most who make the biggest contributions. Strong might say, "Look, we can spend the rest of the year learning everything that anybody knows about this problem, or we can approach it determined to solve it using what we know!" It is hard for me to describe the value of this approach to someone who doesn't already almost understand it, but I know that an aggressive, self-confident approach to a problem can sometimes yield results that will elude the person with the timid approach. And I suppose that the other benefit that I pick out of the many I received from this mentor is not unconnected to this one.

John Strong helped instill a sense of competence and self-confidence in

John Strong (left) and R.W. Wood looking at the new Johns Hopkins engine constructed to rule diffraction gratings (probably in the late 1940s). At that time the gratings from Johns Hopkins were widely used in research spectrometers around the world.

his students. I know many examples of students who, when they finish a Ph.D. research thesis in physics, feel defeated and unsuccessful. They look at the results that came out of their two- or three-year research effort and see that they have loose ends, questions left unanswered, and unattained goals. When any work is organized for publication, the things that have been accomplished are emphasized rather than the blind alleys or the things that have not been done. As a consequence, the results in the published literature seem neater and more complete than they do when viewed from the inside. John Strong helped me to understand that effect.

Of course, my experience with my professor helped shape the approach I took with students some years later when I became the professor. I consider it to be an important part of my job of supervising students' research to help them realize when they have solved a significant problem or gotten a significant result. I have known more than one student to be greatly surprised when I have asked, "Do you realize that you now know something that no one else in the world knows?"

I learned things from John Strong that influenced many parts of my life. I was attempting to state something of his influence, along with that of my father, when I wrote the dedication to my book, *Rainbows, Halos, and Glories.* The way it came out, after a number of tries, was:

> *Dallas Greenler helped me to view the world of nature with an inquiring mind. John Strong helped me develop the tools of science, to enhance my perception of the world. To them, who taught me the pleasures of seeing with the mind as well as the eye, I dedicate this book.*

Was I well along on my way to a significant involvement with the Optical Society? If so, I hadn't a clue. I did attend meetings and give papers on the results of my graduate research, and in that process I first experienced the excitement of being a part of the international community of science. If you share the results of your research at meetings and in published papers, you are connected to the international grapevine through which you hear of the experiment in Stockholm that is being attempted, or the effort that is looking promising in a laboratory in Sapporo. The only way to be a part of that community is by being a participant. It is also true that I was aware of people I knew who had been or became presidents of the OSA. Professor Pfund had been one; John Strong became president two years after I left graduate school; and Bob Hopkins, from Rochester, was president in 1973. But I had taken a different path by going into surface science and had left optics.

I continued to go to an occasional Optical Society meeting over the next few years to talk about the optical insights of how to obtain the infrared spectrum of a very few adsorbed molecules. And, of course, I did talk about optical sky effects—but I needed to be involved in the surface-science community if I were to make any progress there. So I was surprised when, in 1980, Tony DeMaria, then the president of the OSA, called to ask if I would accept the nomination to run for election as a three-year member-at-large of the board of directors. I told him that he had the wrong guy—I was not even in any of the mainstream activities of optics. The only connection was that I seemed to apply some optics to many of the things I worked (or played) at. I didn't even get to most of the annual meetings. It was a flattering offer but clearly a mistake. Tony argued that one of the important functions of the Optical Society was to serve the large community of people with fringe interests in optics (he didn't use the term dilettante, but I could translate) and, in fact, I was a very appropriate example of that community. He did finally convince me that I should be willing to run for election. After all, it was only for a three-year term.

I was elected and served as a member of the board during the time when Bob Madden, who worked at the National Bureau of Standards, was president. Bob was a year ahead of me at Rochester, and although we followed different paths, we ended up at Johns Hopkins as students of John Strong, sharing laboratory space as graduate students.

I did a reasonably conscientious job as board member, doing the necessary homework to be informed on matters that needed to be decided, but I had no administrative ambitions and didn't try to initiate new things or play a leadership role. Scientific societies, such as this one, are an integral part of the scientific enterprise, and it was a most interesting experience to be involved with a group of competent people trying to make the process work as effectively as possible. Although it was a good experience, when my term was up, I was quite willing to quit. I considered that I had done my duty in helping with the infrastructure of science and could now get back to doing the things that had drawn me into a scientific career in the first place.

Thus it was quite a shock when, a year later, I received a call saying that I had been nominated to run for election as vice president, which was the first of an automatic four-year sequence of offices, one of which was the president of the organization. I spent a week debating the pros and cons. The Optical Society at that time had a membership of about ten thousand members, fifteen percent of them from about sixty countries around the world. The organization published eight scientific journals and had an annual budget of about seven million dollars. From my experience on the board I knew how the organization worked, and the only things that made the job seem feasible to me were the excellent Executive Director and the dedicated staff he had assembled. I had known Jarus Quinn when we were both graduate students at Johns Hopkins. He had been Executive Director of the Optical Society for many years, and he efficiently and faithfully carried out the policies that the board of directors established, provided background information when it was needed, and saw to the day-to-day operations of the organization.

I finally decided to accept the nomination and was subsequently elected. Over the next four years I had a number of conversations in which the person I had just met got around to some version of the question, "Well, if your research area is not really optics, how is it that you are the president of the largest optical scientific organization in the world?" I never did figure out how to answer that question.

There are stories of fierce competition in scientific research, and some friends have thought it unlikely that a person gets to be the president of a large scientific organization without significant political activity. But this was not my experience.

I think that there may be two factors involved. At that time my perception was that the Optical Society was a friendly, collegial organization, more so than other scientific groups with which I had contact, and the election process in that organization may have been less politically driven than in other groups.

I know, also, that some of my colleagues consider me to be naive in such matters. Sometimes I do not see the operation of a political process, where to others it is clear. A person who views all group processes as political sees successful interaction within the group to consist of the manipulation of individuals to achieve a desired result. I try not to approach individuals as objects to be manipulated, and so may view the process differently.

So here we are, the board of the Optical Society of America, trying to make a decision that I fear can have some divisive aftereffects if it is not handled carefully.

I have had some experience with the method of "consensus" that Quakers use to make decisions. No vote is taken, and a decision is made only when there is a consensus among everyone present on the course of action. A single dissenter can prevent a decision. For most groups such a method of doing business would be hopeless. However, one of the advantages of the method is that it ensures that every person is able to present his or her viewpoint and to know that it is heard by the group. It seems to me that this feature is so important that it is worth using in other groups where matters are decided by a vote. As a practical matter, taking the time to have each person make his or her argument to the group while having its undivided attention may actually result in the saving of time. A person, given such attention, may need to speak only once, rather than several times in a running argument where interruptions are common and one is never sure of being heard. And if a person knows that his or her ideas have been carefully considered, a contrary decision may be more acceptable.

Each person speaks, some expressing strong feelings about the proposed federation. With the full attention of the group the speeches are shorter than I might have expected. "Please wait with that argument, you will shortly have your chance to develop it fully." Everyone has spoken . . . . "Are there any more comments?" A couple of short rebuttals . . . . "Are we ready for the vote?" Silence all around, and not a little tension . . . . "Those in favor, hold up your hands." The Director counts: one,

two, three, four, five, six, seven, eight votes for the motion. "Those opposed?" One, two, three, . . . six, seven, eight votes against. A moment of silence, then everyone looks at me—and laughs. Because I had said I would not vote, the motion fails. We have done the best we can do.

Chapter Sixteen

THE CAREER

The phone rings. "Hi, Bill. Yes, I have some time to talk. What's up?" What is up is that Bill is planning to retire from his chaired professorship, and his university is considering whom to hire to replace him. He says they want someone with a strong involvement in the teaching of physics who would become the Director of the Center. In addition they are interested in developing the department's involvement in optics research. He says that they have drafted a description of the position, but I am the person for the job, and if I am interested they will rewrite the description to fit whatever I want to do. How about it? Even when I allow for the exaggeration that could result from Bill's enthusiasm, it is a very flattering approach—a significant appointment to an endowed chair at a prestigious private university. How do I respond to that? "Send me the job description. I'll think about it and talk to you again."

The phone call does stir up the question, once again, of where I am headed. In my early days at this developing university in Milwaukee I was on almost all of the important committees. The decision had been made that this institution was going to grow and change dramatically; the only question was whether it was going to grow into a good institution or a mediocre one.

Some of the faculty, understandably enough, resented the change in the ground rules of the place where they had been teaching for some years and decided to dig in their heels to oppose it. Others accepted the changes but did not have the motivation to lead the way. Some joined in to face the new challenges. The decision had been made; the institution was changing. The policies and standards and traditions of the emerging University were being established, and if I didn't contribute my own insights, dreams, biases, and prejudices, then the character of the institution would be shaped by others. It was clear that at no time in the history of this University would an individual faculty member be able to have such an influence on its character.

I was involved in establishing a structure for the awarding of tenure on this campus, in the establishment of an independent Graduate School, and with the building and funding of the Laboratory for Surface Studies, all of which gave me a clear glimpse into the possibility of a career in academic administration. I assumed that if I indicated an interest in becoming an Associate Dean for Sciences in the College of Letters and Sciences, it was likely that I could get such an appointment. If I performed competently in that position, other offers would follow. That career path seemed to be a real possibility. But that is not really where my ambitions lay; I wanted to chase more rainbows.

After nine years on the campus I arranged to spend the 1970-71 academic year working with Norman Sheppard and Dave King in the School of Chemical Sciences at the University of East Anglia in Norwich, England. Before leaving, I resigned from all of the UWM committees. The year gave me the opportunity to be personally involved in research in a stimulating setting, and it also provided much more. It gave me a chance, away from telephone calls, committee meetings, class preparations, and student advising, to think about what I was going to do in the next five or ten years.

I came back to Milwaukee and kept a low profile. The campus had changed greatly in the ten years since I had first joined the faculty. There were now many faculty members with the experience and ambitions to continue shaping the future of this institution. My input seemed less critical; I felt that I had paid some of my dues, and it seemed reasonable for me to spend less time on the University and more on other parts of my career. That is what I really wanted to do.

I had read the book that describes the cynical and humorous ideas of Laurence Peter, all centered around the Principle that took his name. The Peter Principle was featured briefly on the center stage of our pop culture and, after a short overexposure, dropped from sight. But I had the feeling that there was something there to keep in mind. According to the Principle when a person is doing a job at which he is competent, he is, in due time, promoted to the next higher job and given more responsibility. The promotions continue until the person comes to a job at which he is not competent, and he then spends the rest of his career in that job. He has risen to his level of incompetence. The somewhat cynical view of the workplace, then, is that a large fraction of people are stuck in jobs that they are not competent to handle.

If I am to take the responsibility for my career, the way for me to foil the Peter Principle is to somehow avoid that last promotion. If we remove some of the oversimplification, competence and incompetence are not absolute states but lie on the opposite ends of a continuum. The wisdom to be drawn from the Principle lies in my trying to make career choices based not so much on the world's judgment of "success" as on my own judgment of what I am good at doing.

Bill's phone call makes me think of these previous decisions and brings to mind a conversation with a guy I knew when, as a college student, I had a summer job at one of the glass factories in Toledo.

Before I can tell you of the significance of the conversation, I must tell you about the nature of the job.

The job was involved with a pilot-plant production of the new, largest-ever, television tube. This glass tube was made in two parts, a funnel and a face plate, which were later fused together. Each of these parts was made by the same process. First, a big blob of molten glass was dropped into a hot mold. Then, an inner mold was thrust into the glass by a piston with such force that the glass squeezed up to fill all the space between the inner and outer molds. It was an old technique for making pressed-glass products, but no one had ever tried to press such a large glob of glass into such a big piece of glassware as the funnel for this new, seventeen-inch television tube.

The glass was made by a continuous process in which the ingredients were fed into the far end of the furnace and the molten glass was removed at a uniform rate from the end next to the glass-molding machinery. It was important that the furnace input and output remain balanced and constant so that the glass level in the long furnace did not fluctuate. Any small change in that level caused small particles from the fire brick in the walls of the furnace to enter the glass and degrade its quality. To keep the flow uniform, the glass was dispensed, a glob at a time, in equally spaced time intervals.

A piston system disgorged a large glob of glowing glass into a waiting mold. As I recall, the glob weighed something like ten pounds. The mold was one of eight, sitting on a massive table. The table was rotated so that the mold, after receiving the hot glass, was moved under the great hydraulic press carrying the inner mold, which was thrust into the glowing glass. At the same time another glob of glass dropped into the mold behind.

As soon as the inner mold was withdrawn, the table again advanced. Another glob was dropped in a mold, the piston made another thrust, and a newly minted, still-glowing funnel was being cooled by jets of air. As the table rotated two more times, the glass funnel was cooled in its mold until rigid enough to be removed and carried to a nearby furnace. This very hot piece was then placed on a slowly moving belt that carried it through a long annealing furnace. The process kept the glass funnel hot long enough to remove the thermal stresses from its chaotic formation and then allow it to cool slowly to room temperature.

In this pilot-plant operation the design of the molds was being refined and the internal cooling of the inner mold adjusted by the flow of cooling water. Each step had to be adjusted individually: the speed of the thrust, the size of the glass glob, the temperature of the glass, the hundred details which, if wrong, would result in a cracked, nonuniform, or incomplete funnel. My job was to take a variety of data on the temperatures of various parts of the mold and glass just before and just after the pressing process.

This rotating, thumping, hissing, steaming machine had a life of its own that dominated the lives of all of those around it. We had to shout to be heard over its deafening noise. Everywhere the heat was intense. The men carrying those fiercely radiating pieces of glassware to the annealing furnace wore protective clothing but still became so hot that the working rules called for them to carry glass for ten minutes and then sit on a bench, away from the intense heat, for ten minutes. It was another of the rhythms dictated by the machine, ten minutes on duty and ten minutes off. But even that stressful rhythm seemed calm compared with the chaos that replaced it when something went wrong.

All of a sudden one of the molds would not have cooled fast enough and would not release the freshly formed funnel. Desperate attempts to remove it as it paused in position on the next two turns of the table caused it to break. A high-pressure blast of air cleared out some of the glass pieces from the mold, but not all. Time was up. Another glob of glass was dumped in on the remaining pieces.

Quickly we had to stop the hydraulic thrust of the inner mold, or the machine would be damaged. The cooling-air jets would be knocked aside so that a man could twist an iron poker into the molten mass and pull it out of the mold. If he were not quick enough, the mold jumped to the next position, where he tried again. But the same malfunction that caused the one funnel to stick in the mold was repeated on three out of the next four molds, and people were struggling with each one.

The table continued to turn at exact intervals, and the blobs of molten glass continued to fall, precisely on schedule. One of the molds was not cleared even after the second ration of glass was added to the first, and it received yet a third. Now the weight of the glass was great enough that it was difficult to lift even if the man with the poker could engage it firmly enough to pull it free. The flow from the furnace cannot be interrupted. A chute was maneuvered into position to intercept the falling globs and divert them into a container of water. An explosion of steam announced each new contribution. The machine was stopped and the molds were cleared.

Stopping the machine was a serious decision, as it was a complicated procedure to start the machine again. The equilibrium temperature of a mold results from the combination of heating by contact with the hot glass and the internal and external cooling by circulating water and blasts of air. It took a while to reach that equilibrium temperature, and in the meanwhile glass stuck in molds and glass broke. If the problem could be solved without stopping the machine, the operation could be restored quickly.

I got to know one of the guys who carried the hot glass. One day he told me that he had just the job he wanted. He said that when things went wrong and all hell broke loose, he could go over and sit on the bench and wait for the foreman to solve the problem. "He can have the extra pay. I wouldn't take his job if it were offered to me. I've got the job I want!" At the time I was disturbed to think that this young guy would settle for such a lousy job, without any aspirations to do better. Many years later, thinking about the offer of a new position at Bill's university, I view his comments with a different perspective.

A few days after Bill's phone call, I have read the description of the new institute, and I am thinking about his invitation.

> **I realize that the decision made by the glass carrier and the one I am about to make are not so different after all. Each of us, perhaps to avoid the pitfalls of the Peter Principle, decides not to pursue the promotion that will take us to that last level. The main difference is in where we each draw our line. What I really want to be, more than anything else, is a professor at an academic institution. I hope that there will be other good people who will take on the challenges of solving the problems that occur "when all hell breaks loose" so that I can continue to do the job that I want to do—and for which I am most competent. I sit down to write John the letter:**

> Dear John:

> I've read the draft proposal for the Center. You have asked whether I am interested in being considered for the Center's endowed chair. The question itself is a compliment that I appreciate. An endowed chair at the Center is not something that I can dismiss out of hand, but since you have talked with me about it, I have given it much careful thought and conclude that, in spite of its many advantages, it is not the move I want to make. I hope you find the right person for the position; it could be a very significant appointment.

Chapter Seventeen

CHASING THE RAINBOW

My new *Science Bag* program opens this Friday, and I still haven't got the rainbow screen made. I've practiced and found out how to do it; Barbara has sewn together a ten-foot-square of dark blue cloth for me, but I still have to attach the tiny glass beads that will produce the dazzling rainbow in the lecture room. Today is the day. I obtained the beads I need by buying a fifty-pound bag of the small glass beads that are used by the highway department to make painted, highway-marking stripes reflective. Whenever I work with the beads, some seem to escape and spread over the floor, so I will take the screen outside for this operation.

Over next to the Engineering Building on campus is a corner sheltered on two sides from the light wind. That should be a good place to lay out the big cloth. I spray a section of it with adhesive, then pick up the kitchen salt-shaker filled with the glass beads and proceed to sprinkle them over the sticky surface. The sun is shining on the cloth, and when I move to the right position, I see a section of a beautiful, intense bow formed by the sunlight and the tiny glass spheres. Tremendous! This is really going to work very well. As I spray and sprinkle, clouds cover the sun and the bow disappears. I have lost my quality control over the job, but it should still work okay.

Spray and sprinkle, spray and sprinkle . . . . A wind comes up, eddies around the corner of the building, and picks up the little pile of dried leaves and candy wrappers and cigarette butts that I had noticed in the corner. The tiny whirlwind of this debris moves across my screen, leaving a line of trash across the sticky cloth. Nuts. I pick off the bigger pieces and proceed, spray and sprinkle, spray . . . . the wind comes again and the trash devil crosses—and recrosses—my cloth. I should have realized the meaning of that little heap of leaves in the corner. I think that I have picked this particular cigarette filter tip off the cloth three times now. More and more garbage is getting left on my cloth. Here it comes again. Okay, I give up.

Get a broom, scrub all the debris and the glass beads off the cloth, and start over. Take it inside to an empty room, spray and sprinkle till it is covered with beads, let it dry, carefully roll up the finished rainbow screen, and then vacuum up the glass beads that got away. That should do it.

I have been chasing rainbows for much of my life. The chase has had its benefits, and it has had its costs. What costs? The most obvious is the limitation it has placed on what I have been able to achieve in surface science, my "serious" research. Of course, I am using rainbows as a metaphor for sky effects, butterfly wings, *Science Bags*, spinning tops— all of those things that the NSF program director had implied in the Washington-Berlin telephone call that I should give up if I were to expect to get continuing support for my surface-science work.

The organization of my life determines that more time spent on one activity means less spent on some other. It is also true that the nature of the teaching-learning-organizing-researching-consulting-professoring enterprise is such that a few extra hours per week significantly affect the scientific output of the enterprise. In the language of financial analysts, my research output is highly leveraged. So time spent chasing rainbows has had, I'm sure, a significant impact on what I've been able to achieve in surface science. Where has this left me in the catalog of scientific achievement?

To answer this question, I might try to make something of a letter sent to me from Ireland with the address written exactly like this:

PROF. R. GREENLER
PRESIDENT
UNIVERSITY OF WISCONSIN
U.S.A.

The fact that someone in Ireland would think this to be an adequate address might suggest that they thought I was rather well known. And the fact that it was actually delivered to me in Milwaukee might suggest that they were right. Some of the other facts, however, might also be relevant. The "President" label was apparently some remnant of my recent presidency of the Optical Society. The University of Wisconsin label got it delivered to the campus in Madison where, presumably, someone in the mailroom decided that, although R. Greenler was not known to be the University President, it might be worth checking the directory to see who this individual was.

An R. Greenler was listed as working at the Center for Biology Education, and so it was forwarded to Robin Greenler, my daughter. When she opened it and saw that it contained information for traveling to Ireland, she dismissed it as another of those travel promotions that clutter our mail. She was about to drop it into the basket when she remembered that her father had said something about being invited to give a talk in Ireland, and she examined the address more carefully—and decided to send it on to me in Milwaukee. The weakest link in the chain may have been the last, when it had been delivered to a member of my own family and had almost been discarded. Fame has it limits.

By my own, home-made ranking scale I would say that I am a third-rank scientist. On this scale, the first rank consists of those who have received international recognition for their major contributions to science, sometimes marked by their receiving of major awards, such as the Nobel Prize. For many their work has a flavor of something that smacks, if not of genius, certainly of brilliance.

The second rank might be those people who are well-known in the scientific community for their abundant scientific achievements, who are elected to the National Academy of Sciences in the United States or become Fellows of the Royal Society in England (to name only two examples), and who frequently occupy leadership positions in the international science establishment.

The third rank would consist of people who are well known within the international community of their own specialty research area, who are invited to present their work at conferences, who are asked to review papers for publications and grant proposals, and who have received some recognition from scientific organizations.

Even a third-rank scientist has dreams of the lucky discovery that would result in a Nobel Prize, and he might be hesitant to admit that it was probably only a fantasy. If I had concentrated more single-mindedly on research in one area, would I have produced more scientific results and had a greater sense of accomplishment from it? Probably so. Would I have risen to the second rank of scientists? I don't know—very possibly not.

There is a German scientist whom I have known for years. I like him and am glad to run into him at scientific meetings, and yet I have felt an unease in his presence. I have always been somewhat overawed by his scientific accomplishments and his superior understanding of things in the field where our interests overlap.

A few years ago when I saw him at a meeting, I opened the conversation with a question different from the usual one. I asked him what activities in his life were giving him some satisfaction. The resulting conversation was different from our usual exchange; it had a softer tone. He spoke of his wife and son and family relationships. He talked about his recreations as well as his professional efforts. He described a large laboratory involving quite a number of people, all of whom depended on him for financial support as well as scientific leadership. And, although his work was going well, there was a hint of his feeling trapped by the success.

Then he said something that left me flabbergasted. He said that he admired my involvement in rainbows and butterfly wings, that he had no such activity in his life, and that I was fortunate to have developed such interests. I was amazed; it was not something I had expected to hear. No doubt there was some of the green-grass effect involved, but it made me take another look at the cost/benefit balance of some of the choices I had made.

There was a time, before science had become a profession and had been sorted into separate disciplines, when the appropriate subjects of investigation for a natural philosopher included anything that caught his or her interest. John Tyndall, an Irish scientist who was appointed Professor of Natural Philosophy at the Royal Institution in 1853, is one of several examples who comes to mind. Although he was perhaps the first prominent natural philosopher to call himself a physicist, his investigations ranged widely over what we would now call physics, geology, physical chemistry, and bacteriology.

Tyndall followed Michael Faraday at the Royal Institution and continued, in Faraday's tradition, to present popular, informative, and enjoyable lecture demonstrations to the public. For reasons not entirely clear Tyndall seems to be a person who has not received the recognition he merits for his very considerable accomplishments. I know some Irish scientists who also feel that Ireland gets little credit for the accomplishments of this distinguished Irishman, because he spent most of his professional life in England.

Tyndall, a dedicated mountain climber, developed a number of interests in geology, including the flow of glaciers and the action of geysers. He applied his insights on the scattering of light to phenomena in many different areas. He understood the light-scattering process that produces the blue color of the sky—a process sometimes called Tyndall scattering although the mathematical treatment by Lord Rayleigh usually results in it now being called Rayleigh scattering. From his understanding came his prediction that space would appear black to an observer who could get outside the earth's atmosphere. Although he was not the first to demonstrate the function of a light pipe, he did predict that the effect would be used in communication, as it is now used in fiber optics.

He once and for all disposed of the idea of "spontaneous generation" by a set of ingenious experiments. He showed that meat or meat broth would not spoil, even in contact with the air, if all the small particles were trapped and removed from the air that contacted the meat. In the Royal Institution today there are samples of meat and meat broth that he sterilized and sealed in glass tubes—one hundred and twenty years ago—that have not spoiled.

In more recent times there are still a few examples of scientists who have made contributions in a variety of fields, but the organization of science today does not encourage such a diversity of scientific interests; chasing the rainbow is not the recommended path for a person who dreams of making his or her mark in science. I have mentioned some of the costs of such an approach but, of course, there are benefits also.

For me one of the benefits has been the possibility of sharing ideas with people in different parts of the university. I count seven different departments in my university where I have given colloquium talks. In Physics, of course, I have talked about many things; in Geosciences, about atmospheric optical effects; in Chemistry, about surface science and also about beautiful sky effects; in Biology, about iridescent colors in biological organisms; in Psychology, about visual perception; in Music, about the way musical instruments work; and in Art, about the description and perception of color and also about sky effects. That list suggests a web of connections that makes me feel very much a part of the broader university community.

Other benefits come from the diversity of experience that results from the rainbow chase. Each different activity holds the possibility of unanticipated pleasures. For me the Antarctic experience was a bonus resulting from one of my involvements that started as "nonserious" science. I will give one example of a trivial incident in Antarctica that enriches my life. One day, on my first trip to the South Pole research tation, I walked over to the copper pipe that was driven into the ice to mark, as closely as possible, the actual position of the earth's rotation axis—the real South Pole. I have never felt that I understand, well enough, the international date line or the effect of being able to step from one day into another when you cross that imaginary line. It is hard to put my finger on exactly what it is I don't understand about the date line; when I think about it, I can figure out the answer to any question I can formulate. But I am still left with the uneasy feeling there is something there that I don't understand very well.

While standing near that copper pipe, I positioned myself so that I was standing on the line of longitude that passes through New Zealand, and my watch then told me the time and date in New Zealand. Because our airplane contact came from New Zealand, the Pole Station, as a matter of convenience, runs on New Zealand time. As I walked slowly in a counterclockwise circle around that copper pipe marking the pole, I kept reciting the time to myself as I stepped into each new time zone. Here I start at ten o'clock in the morning, here it is nine o'clock, here eight, seven, ... three, two, one, midnight, and here eleven o'clock in the evening—of yesterday—ten, nine, eight, ... three, two, one, noon, eleven in the morning. Just before I arrive back to the longitude of New Zealand I step across the International Date Line and jump back to today. In a real sense I have just walked around the world.

I was so taken by that idea that, after looking around to see that nobody was watching, I continued to walk around the earth, counterclockwise, seven times, to see what effect it would have on me. If someone can't see why that incident enriches my life, I'm afraid that I have no way of explaining it.

There is a way in which I have done some rainbow chasing within the field of surface science. I have usually worked in areas where not many other scientists are working, always a bit out of the mainstream. I have been fortunate to get modest funding to pursue the areas that have interested me rather than following those that were in vogue with funding agencies. A person starting out in an experimental science today operates under greater constraints. The amount of money available for fundamental research in many areas is decreasing. More and more emphasis is placed on research directed toward solving society's problems, and an increasing fraction of what is available for fundamental research is being put into "Big Science" projects, projects that involve large facilities and large teams of scientists. Congress may consider that science is well supported when they put twenty billion dollars toward a space station; many of the scientists that I know would argue that the same amount of money would yield tremendously richer returns if it were invested in "Small Science," where it could support tens of thousands of individual research projects.

I suspect that if I were starting my research career now, the choices I made would not allow me to compete successfully for scarce funding and to have a viable career in a research-oriented university. The NSF project director's admonition, that I would have to concentrate my efforts more if I expected to be supported by his division, might well be something a young researcher cannot now ignore.

The opening night program of "Rainbows, Visible and Invisible" is going as well as opening nights go. I show a collection of rainbow pictures while talking about the rainbow myths and legends that have appeared in almost every culture. These are attempts to explain both the origin and the meaning of this marvelous arch of color that appears in the sky. I move on to Descartes' explanation, talk about the supernumerary bows, discuss the light inside the bow, show more rainbow photos, and point out how many more things they can now see in these pictures than in the first ones I showed them. Now, I demonstrate the rainbow produced by one drop (water in a spherical flask) . . . talk about how to show the bow produced by twenty billion drops (glass beads) . . . tell about the problem of trying to show the whole rainbow to a big audience (the solution is to put the light source close to the drops and locate the observers further away) . . . tell about the problem of trying to make the rainbow cloth earlier in the week . . . the wind, clouds, and the whirlwind of trash . . . show the rainbow . . . beautiful . . . they love it.

On the day of opening night, after I had finally succeeded in putting the beads on the cloth, I had an idea. I could tell the audience about the difficulty of making the rainbow screen, and then, after the demonstration, I could retell the story in different terms.

Suppose I tell you the same story as I told you before, about the rainbow cloth and my difficulty with the wind and debris, but tell it in the form it might take after being passed on by a few generations of storytellers to their listeners sitting around their campfires. It might come out something like this:

"Once there was a man who loved rainbows. He said to himself, 'Why don't I make a rainbow cloth that will let me have a rainbow any time the sun shines?' He liked the idea so much that he proceeded to attach droplets to his cloth. The rainbow's friend, the wind, seeing the bow starting to appear in the cloth, was afraid that this man would forever trap the rainbow in his magic cloth, and so, to protect her friend, she blew clouds over the sun. Without the sun the man could not catch the rainbow in his cloth. But he persisted in his ways, preparing the magic cloth to catch the bow when the sun again appeared. But the wind refused to give up. She picked up leaves and debris and, again and again, dropped them over the cloth, until the man, finally defeated, gave up, took his cloth, and went away."

Yes, I've heard legends that sound like that.

But as I think about it later, the part of the story that I want most to tell is that the man showed his magic cloth to many people, who marveled at the beauty of the colors and who were fascinated by their new-found understanding of how that bow came to be. And these people searched the sky, and when they next saw the rainbow, following the storm, they saw it with fresh eyes. They saw things in the sky that they had never seen before, and the rainbow was more wonderful to them than it had ever been. And then the man thought that the time spent making his rainbow cloth had not been wasted.

For Further Reading

For readers who are interested in learning more about some of the topics covered in this book, I suggest the following:

Rainbows, Halos, and Glories by Robert Greenler. New York: Cambridge University Press, 1980, reissued Milwaukee: Peanut Butter Publishing, 1999. This earlier book describes in more detail many of the optical sky effects referred to in the current volume.

Atmospheric Halos by Walter Tape. Washington D.C.: American Geophysical Union, 1994. This book, with fifty beautiful color photos, concentrates on sky effects that are produced by ice crystals in the atmosphere.

The Nature of Light and Color in the Open Air by Marcel Minnaert. Translated from the Dutch by H. M. Kraemer-Priest and revised by K. E. Brian Jay. New York: Dover, 1954. A more recent version of this book, titled *Light and Color in the Outdoors*, is a translation with some revision by Len Seymour and contains a beautiful set of photographs by Pekka Parviainen and some of his Finnish colleagues; New York: Springer-Verlag, 1993. Minnaert's book, discussed in Chapter Four, is a treasure trove of information about naked-eye observations in our world.

Color and Light in Nature by David Lynch and William Livingston. New York: Cambridge University Press, 1995. This beautifully illustrated book treats a wide range of naturally occurring optical effects seen with the naked eye.

Sunsets, Twilights, and Evening Skies by Aden and Marjorie Meinel. New York: Cambridge University Press, 1983. The title describes the focus of this book on observable optical phenomena in nature. Many striking photographs capture the effects described.

Michael Faraday and the Royal Institution by John Meurig Thomas. Bristol: IOP Publishing Ltd., 1991. This book, by a director of the Royal Institution of Great Britain, tells the remarkable story of the man who shaped the development of that Institution and made the fundamental discoveries that underlie much of twentieth-century technology.

John Tyndall: Essays on a Natural Philosopher, edited by W. H. Brock, N. D. McMillan, and R. C. Mollan. Dublin: The Royal Dublin Society, 1981. This collection of essays describes the great breadth of interest and accomplishment of this Victorian scientist who could also be described as a Renaissance man.

Look forward to *The Rainbow Bridge: Rainbows in Art, Myth, and Science* by Raymond L. Lee and Alistair B. Fraser. This 430-page tome has been in preparation for several years and is scheduled to be published by Penn State University Press in the spring of 2001.

Science Bag videotapes are available through Blue Sky Associates by calling (262) 377-1398. For a description of these tapes and other educational products, see the web page at www.blueskyassociates.com.

Biography

Robert Greenler is an Emeritus Professor of Physics at the University of Wisconsin-Milwaukee, where he has been a member of the faculty since 1962. He was instrumental in the development of the Laboratory for Surface Studies at the University.

In 1988 Dr. Greenler received the Millikan Lecture Award from the American Association of Physics Teachers "for creative teaching of physics." He served as president of the Optical Society of America in 1987 and in 1993 received the Society's first Esther Hoffman Beller Award for "extraordinary leadership in advancing the public appreciation and understanding of science."

In January 1977 Dr. Greenler was at the U.S. Antarctic Research Station at the South Pole studying optical sky phenomena and the ice crystals that cause them. He pursued this research in the Arctic at Point Barrow, Alaska, in March 1978 and returned to the South Pole in December 1997, and again in November 1998, to continue this investigation.

Dr. Greenler also has made an important impact on science education. He has taught courses for high school and middle school teachers and has promoted science education in the classroom as well as informal science education for the public. He is the organizer and, until recently, director of *The Science Bag*, a series of public science programs at the University of Wisconsin-Milwaukee. Since the advent of *The Science Bag* in 1973 over 120,000 people have participated. He has produced a series of twenty-six videotapes of selected *Science Bag* programs, which are being used in classrooms and museums around the country.

Dr. Greenler and his wife, Barbara, a retired psychotherapist, live in Mequon, Wisconsin. They are the parents of three grown children and grandparents of six grandchildren.

Chasing the
RAINBOW
RECURRENCES IN THE LIFE OF A SCIENTIST

To order copies of *Chasing the Rainbow* and/or *Rainbows, Halos, and Glories,* please complete the form below. (Please feel free to duplicate this form.)

Chasing the Rainbow
Hardcover _____copies at $34.95 per copy $ _____
Paperback _____copies at $25.95 per copy $ _____

Rainbows, Halos, and Glories
Paperback _____copies at $29.95 per copy) $ _____

Sales Tax   (Wisconsin Residents add 5.6%) $ _____

Shipping and Handling $ _____
    ($4.00 for first book; $1.00 for each additional book)

Total Amount Enclosed $ _____

Checks should be made payable to: Blue Sky Associates.

Ordered By:

Name: _____

Address:_____

City: _____

State: _____   Zip: _____

Phone Number: (_____) _____

❏ Please send me a catalog of educational material offered by Blue
    Sky Associates

Complete this order form and mail it to:

Blue Sky Associates
920 Seventh Avenue, Grafton, WI 53024
262-377-1398
www.blueskyassociates.com